MW01141021

The Words Wanting Out

Poems Selected & New

THE WORDS WANTING OUT

POEMS SELECTED & NEW

BARRY DEMPSTER

For Anita, Sean + Isolde,
thank you so much for
your Victoria hospitality!
Wishing you the very
best of words.

Barry
May/2004

NIGHTWOOD EDITIONS

ROBERTS CREEK, BC

2003

Copyright © Barry Dempster, 2003

ALL RIGHTS RESERVED. The use of any part of this publication reproduced, transmitted in any form or by any means, electronic, mechanical, photocopying, recording, or otherwise, or stored in a retrieval system, without the prior written consent of the publisher – or, in the case of photocopying or other reprographic copying, a licence from the Canadian Copyright Licensing Agency – is an infringement of the copyright law.

Nightwood Editions
R.R. #22, 3692 Beach Ave.
Roberts Creek, BC
V0N 2W2, Canada

Edited for the house by Silas White
Typesetting by Carleton Wilson

We gratefully acknowledge the support of the Canada Council for the Arts and the British Columbia Arts Council for our publishing program.

NATIONAL LIBRARY OF CANADA CATALOGUING IN PUBLICATION

Dempster, Barry, 1952–
    The words wanting out : poems selected & new / Barry Dempster.

ISBN 0-88971-192-5

    I. Title.

PS8557.E4827W67 2003   C811'.54   C2003-905734-8

CONTENTS

SECTION I

SECTION 2

SECTION 3

SECTION 4

SECTION 5

SECTION I

BOOKS ARE

Books do not breathe, or
share your soup, stroke your
arms, inhale your rare perfumes.
Books do not spit, love or scheme
for more. Books do not live
parallel lives. Books do not
pray or hold mirrors unto God.
Books do not die with regrets.

What books do is talk
endlessly. Not to you or
the sycamores or the china
cups, but to no avail at all.
Talk, more talk. Books have
something to say and are bound
to say it. Books equal
their words exactly.

Since my last letter I have
been a book or several books
together. I do not listen
or spit. I talk to thin air.

Books are and emphasize.
Nothing, they chant and storm
will ever stay the same. The
wind on everything, pages
turned, pages torn.

LINKS

She plays the piano, her head
folded into her bosom like a flower.
He sits beside her, the edge of one
thigh pressed on the gathers of
her dress. Chopin in the air. Summer
night tinkling. The parlour heavy with warm thoughts.

There are lovely words in his mouth, his
cheeks stuffed with candy hearts. *Run away
with me into the forest, we'll live in a cabin,
sleep on pine boughs.* His throat is tight,
the collar of his hard shirt like a lock.
Moon shines on the piano keys, turns into music.

She is so innocent, pale eyes closed, one
foot tapping discreetly. A wolf howls out
back. She thinks it romantic – the hot
fur, growls trembling, wet, white teeth
dazzling like stars. He hears it too,
dreams of protecting her.

When they rise, she catches a glimpse of
herself in the mirror: tiny, wedding-party pink,
waist slim enough for fingers. She brushes against
him, sends him into the night steaming.
There's a strip of light on the road – he rides his
horse as if it were time, pounding into the future.

When they're married, they both imagine babies.
My mother is born during dinner one night.
Then I'm there, wanting to be. I learned from
my grandfather how to beat time. They look at
me, then down at their baby, a sixty-year-old
woman with blue hair. Grandmother turns to dust.

I place their bones on the piano bench, link them
together like chains. Music fills the room. His leg
bone lies over her thigh, his fingers like sticks wrapped
around her waist. Picking my mother up, I leave,
down the same shining road, horse hooves mixed
with the howling of a piano.

PARASITES

Parasites, my family living off Scarborough
like bacteria thriving in red silky lungs.
It's the peace, my mother said, *how heavenly*,
her nervous fingers flitting through flower beds,
killing lilies and violets along with the weeds.
A haven for Dad to hide his awful childhood,
a workbench, a driveway, a compost heap.
While I, little tapeworm, blindly burrowed
in the flesh of a lonely only child,
a thinness known as luck and security.
When my favourite aunt came to visit,
she joked about glistening cemetery lawns,
the dead basking on top of their tombstones
like fallen angels or careless leprechauns.
My country cousin was reminded of meadows
trimmed with fingernail scissors
and smoothed by the hands of a thousand saints.
Heavenly, my Nana agreed, the cumbersome past
shrunk to the size of a two-bedroom bungalow
miraculous with oil heat and washing machine.
Suburban salvation, TV antennae
sending songs to God, all the grateful cuckoos
squeezed in their tiny, temporary nests.

SUNDAY SCHOOL AND THE PROMISED LAND

In Sunday school, Christ's hometown
was every colour in a crayon box,
from the strawberry red noses
of the donkeys, to the ink black
winter skies. Israel was the
Promised Land, a temporary title
like Miss America or the Stanley Cup,
before God moved his whole caravan
to North America, destination
the Scarborough Gospel Hall.
The Old Testament
crawled across deserts, through seas,
sprawling breathless in the Bay of Fundy,
bumming a ride to Toronto
in the back of a livestock truck.
The Gentiles pressed their ears
to the chocolate coloured ground
and heard the new centre of the earth.

Matthew, Mark, Luke and John wrote
words white as sheets. *They're talking
to you*, my Sunday school teacher claimed,
a little boy who felt less solid
than Casper the Friendly Ghost.
From Bethlehem to Golgotha to
a Brethren Gospel Hall on Warden Ave.
When Christ was a child like me
he loved to ride the streetcars,
his shoulder-length hair drifting
in the breeze. He sang
his daily "God Save the Queen"
and hid most of his Christmas cake
in a balled-up serviette.
Every Sunday he memorized psalms,
watching slides of faraway children
better known as heathens; exactly
like me, wondering why God had chosen him
while leaving the rest of the world wild.

POEMS HOME, AN ONLY CHILDHOOD

1. *Hernia*

I don't like it here   the light smells   the bed beanstalk tall
the nurses filing their nails to needles   the window a
brown brick wall. I see a boy in the hall who looks like a
long pink scar   his eyes shut tight as mouths. How do
they get away with it   keeping kids in cages   cutting them
up? I dream of Dad with a ladder leaned against his solid
shoulders like a burgled house. *Just relax love*   says the
flashlight in the middle of the night. And before I know
it a masked men dressed in fluorescent white is shaking
me by the veins. To count to ten is all uphill and me a
whiz in every corner of Miss McLaren's class. A sudden
witch's face   *We're going to snip your peter off*. Another
dream of Dad digging in the garden   all the way to
Chinatown. Then nothing   sweet nothing   the clean
colourless walls of the scariest sleep. When I finally wake
I feel as stiff and abandoned as a killed cat. Peter hasn't
gone and I can count to a zillion again   but the light still
smells and the nurses swear behind their teeth. What a
way to rid the world of little boys   scars carrying them
away like ships.

2. *The Maple*

Six years old   the backyard like a playpen with its soft
flowers and slat fence. I can somersault the length of it in
half a minute. I can practically pick the entire lawn blade
by blade   a mere bouquet. There isn't even room to
invent an older brother. Or for baseball bats to swing   or
paper airplanes   or secret hideaways. Except for one giant
red maple middle of the puniness   rising to a hundred-
watt sun and a front-row seat in space. Branches enough
for a big extended family   imagination's field day.
Halfway up is where I first discover fences repeating
themselves   yard after yard of trapped kids tumbling

restlessly   fists full of plucked grass. No way to camouflage this longing   my brain cells bursting through the neighbourhood. Goodbye violets and pansies   adios cracks and slats. A red-maple sky teeming with children's eyes.

3. *Birchmount Pool*

Summer mornings   8 AM the pool still nippy from the night before   the colour of a chain-link fence. Look at all of us   frozen eight-year-olds   twisting into wrinkled bathing trunks   chewing on our Batman towels. One by one   lining up in the shadow of a diving board   a great unsteady slab of fear. From the first dawn when I hold my nose and bubble   to my premiere cannonball   I brave a hundred cold gulps of death. But a gangplank is too much to ask   a pirate of a push into mid-air. I know that a belly flop can split a child in two. I can hear the thump of a head hitting bottom. How can I bounce across the board when I am so well-read   knowing anyone can drown in just a glass of water? *Teacher   Teacher   I am excusing myself*   my toes curling over the top step   my lungs stuffed with deep gasps of gravity. Counting my way back down to calmness   already planning a whale of a story to break my parents' hearts. *You see they hold me under   won't let me out to pee   they make me swim by pinching me.* My mother always believes in cruelty   never wanting me to leave the house again. These spine-chilling stories diving from great dramatic heights   dropping the world on its head.

4. *Aunt Marguerite*

Aunt Marguerite is a Simpson's clerk   wrapping packages pleating bows   pretending every single day is an occasion. At home her pleasures are all comic-book big   a grand piano   a solid oak buffet   a bear-sized rocking chair   a china cabinet bursting with gold-rimmed cups and platters. Too much my mother says   like she's trying to fill a galaxy. Even the grandfather clock is bigger than boredom   big enough for me to mirror the swinging pendulum   my shoulders swaying halfway to the floor. Not even a crybaby can pout at Aunt Marguerite's   she dries your eyes with two-fisted chunks of gingerbread cake. And how about this jumbo horseshoe hassock   troubles galloping off into endless horizons. Nothing better than wrapping an ordinary day in sheets and sheets of Aunt Marguerite   playing hide-and-seek with the vases chasing an octave across the room   rocking the bear. Pretending every stick of furniture conceals the tall-tale memories of a tree.

5. *Marnie*

C'mon   it's not like I haven't seen one before   Marnie taunts her pointing finger stabbing like a knife at the waistband of my underpants. Marnie who has seen her older brother buck-naked a billion times. She looks a bit like a panda with all that white skin glaring against her tan. Oh for a keyhole or a telescope   where I can watch without her watching me. Like now   Marnie's beady eyes bearing down on my crotch   her fingernails in the shape of a pluck. An only child has a calling for privacy   born with one shy paw cupping my balls. It takes a ruthless girl like Marnie for me to pull down my pants   my thighs trembling like snapped elastic   a piece of me petrified   a one-eyed glaze of a stare. Baring   just dangling there until I can stuff what no longer entirely belongs to me back into its cold pouch   catching a last glimpse of Marnie bending into her panties   a flash of red like a tongue sticking out.

6. *Prob's Bush*

Born with an hourly bulletin in my brain   *Stay away from Prob's bush or else.* Mother   protecting her only one with tales of greenish clouds full of poison-ivy gas   and perverts who lurk behind logs   sniffing the marshmallow ankles of disobedient boys. But Prob's Bush is the only wilderness I know   brooks and skinny birches   bottom-heavy skunks and sandpapery weeds   caves and mud crickets and caterpillar guck. How the old ladies wrap themselves in black shawls just outside the path   park benches like stone dogs guarding the gates to Hell. Each entry a lungful of precious breath   a horse's plunge over a fiery cliff   a gravedigger's final hole. If I can survive the burrs   the bugs   the porcupine barbs   then I can surely outlast my mother's lonely fears. An only child needs a birchbark note excusing him from his only mom and dad. Just one more wildness in the wilderness   one more caterpillar leg. Just another eyeball in the brook   another rash. Even the perverts can't tell me apart from all the other kids. As they chase me over rock and slime   I feel as free as the strength slipping from a strong man's fist   a grip broken into a thousand pieces.

7. *Robin's House*

Robin's house is the life I don't have   a million dishes in the murky kitchen sink   dustballs the size of hand grenades   dog turds on the suspiciously slippery basement floor. The stuff of rare diseases   fever sweats and skin eruptions. After a day with Robin my mother boils me until my crevices unfold. But cleanliness is just another word for solitude. Spotless and lonely   couches without a crease   coffee tables as deep as the Dead Sea chandeliers that glisten like a huddle of homeless stars. If only my mother could follow me to Robin's house   the cobwebs kissing her cheekbones   old newspapers warming her toes   the smell of a grandad and several little sisters reassuring her she never has to be alone. At Robin's house we roll back and forth across the carpet until we are plastered with dog hairs and cookie crumbs   bobby pins and scum   the stuff of overflowing families   layers of love.

HOUSEWORK

Mother is out before anyone
in the sand-shining dawn, stringing
wet clothes on dewy clotheslines.
The sky is bleary, an eye
still filled with sleep.
She sails bright things into the yard,
coloured clouds over the dim grass.
By the time sun has broken through,
mother is sitting on the porch, coffee steaming,
her family dancing over the golden lawn.

The kitchen is thick with smells.
Close your eyes; they become
entire rooms to breathe. Mother is poised
over the stove, stirring whirlpools
in soup as if frozen, the same motion
over and over – spoon in a
scented ocean, bubbles rising to burst.
We watch, quiet, patient over
china bowls, swallowing food memories.

Folding clean linen, curling dust
in the shaggy mop, heart attached to arms,
she scrubs and scours, smoke racing up
the chimney, leaving nothing behind but gleams.
At night we hear her peeling off clothes
in her bedroom, a sigh – listen for the thump
her body will make when it hits the bed.
It doesn't. Drifting, like a ball of dust,
she lifts herself before she lands.

THE DARKEST HOUR

The sweatiest hour of the night, dreams
raiding the Bible for gruesome props, a plaque
of John 3:16 falling on my pillow
like an axe, the small collection of Sunday
bow ties snapping around my wrists and ankles.
If I were to open my inner eyes
Christ would be stacking crosses in my heart,
just the normal order, a lifetime supply.
If I were to wake up, the moon would look
crucified across the venetian blinds, the
whole room a reflection of slow, certain death.

In school when asked to draw a typical
day, my entire page was orange, the sun
concealing everything. I was somewhere
in the glare of it all, an inconsequential
spark. No one had to know I was religious,
burning up I blended in, just as the
Bible had always warned. Wide awake,
the sun obliterated every shadow,
changing even the chimneys
into harmless waverings of light.

ARITHMETIC

Arithmetic taught me loads
about oranges and apples
and some kid named Billy
who was always dividing and subtracting them
amongst his lucky friends.
Just like world economy, same shape,
same sharing, only
those fruits are made of gold.

What about the tattered
woman sitting on Bloor Street
in front of Harry Rosen's walking sticks
and tweed caps, a cardboard sign
propped up beside her asking for spare cash?
If I give her half a handful, then go in
and give Harry my right arm and left ball,
how much of me will make it home?

It's the deep-freeze part of me
that shivers as the bank machine
slips me a sandwich of green bills.
I was never very good at math, gave away
far too much of myself. And now
I'm supposed to hoard the higher numbers
of bonds and GICs, those paper mansions
guaranteeing a future gleam.

One look is all I can spare,
most of my vision in a vault somewhere.
Walking the downtown streets, eyes
half-closed, both the beggars and the shoppers
flip past, the green queens in my wallet,
a hidden *Village of the Damned.*

Inside of me where nothing
is supposed to last, a small-
nonetheless-suffering beggar sits,
his arms held out, palms waiting.
I give him everything, all the dreams
I can muster, promises by the pound,
until his little fingers are leaking gold.
Still he keeps begging.

How many oranges, how many apples?
Dreams and promises! Paper money
multiplies with each bundle tossed in the air.
The mannequins in Harry Rosen's window
are handing out things to wear.

SOMEWHERE . . .

LONDON 1910

From the cloudy bustle of Charing Cross
the stairs greet paradise in a
great tiger's eye of electric
lights; where expectations unite.

Women with their perfumed waggeries
stream from silky stores. Bookshop
windows wink with expensive paper
while theatre marquees sweep down
across the streets like velvet capes.

On the edge of discovery
narrow lanes veering into frilly squares
zooming their way through
circuses and parks. Round every corner
another corner leading to eternity.

Mr. Hueffer breaks his literary bread
in the whirr of Trafalgar Square.
Critics crowd the Tower gates
and call gloriously for heads.
Oh, newsprint afternoons
the city castled in books.
Mr. Lawrence walks like a royal verb.

The perfect city is a swoon
done up in essences and trimmed
with metaphors. I am wobbling
in pleasure, my eyes thrilled wide.
The never-dared made drunk.

Somewhere on a haunted street
deadman Dickens writes impressions
in the energetic air. The sentence
carries on. Somewhere a white peacock
speaks its rarity to all sorts of men.
The deed is done, just waiting to be written.

London, halfway between the earth
and moon . . . men like me trotting
on the light, trying to toss
reflections on an unsuspecting world.
Each silver street
rounding out the future.

HIPPIES

The slurred boogie of Volkswagen
vans came to a stop in the field
across from our house. Tall, lanky
melodies spilled out onto the grass
with their guitars and wide-eyed women.
One girl had stars pinned on her ears.
Another wore flowers instead of brassiere.

I started dressing in dirty denim
and a pair of my mother's beads.
I'd sit on the safe side of our hedge, trying
to look cool, but they never made a move.

At night they built yellow mounds
of fire, singing Dylan songs,
rising up to my window,
whirling me around the room.
My mother began locking me in
like one of the valuables.

The police arrived on the third night,
busting up a chorus of "Like a Rolling Stone."
They were gone, like ghosts,
before dawn, heading off to
the pink horizon.

And then somewhere, in a fresher field,
they settled in, prancing about like
elves, tempting another dreamy boy.

In my field, they left
the black circles of what once
was light and on one lone tree
they drew a figure of an angel
braiding daisies in the hair of God.

UNCLE CLAUDE

it was always over a game
of crazy eights   around the kitchen
table   the night the size of a
closet   a part of me would
rise   like the smoke from your
cigarette   drifting across the table
getting mixed up with your hands
in your eyes   there i was   forming
a child around your head.

your cigarette ashes dropped methodically
into heaps in the ashtray   you made
sure of it   same time dealing as
fast as a gambler   cracking jokes
making miracles out of the cards
between your yellow man-sized fingers.

i was obsessed with your eyes   the
coils of tight colour   flashing around
the room   your skull of short white
hair   the wrinkles on your forehead
like years unravelling   your prowess
the way   with a smile   you handled
little boys   cigarettes   a pack of cards.

now when i see you   too tired after
supper for games   flopped on the couch
like a pillow   old eyes stuck to the
TV set   night leaning on your shoulders
i almost forget how big you once were
next to me   how cool with your talent
your affection   the memory gleaming
dull as a quarter moon   as tentative as smoke.

TO GRANT (A FAMILIAR VERB)

Grant, godson of Seabrights Bay, water-skis
like Christ smoothing over waves. He
flies, he veers, he writes his name
across the shore. This comes easy
for a man, one foot lifted in the air.
Except for me, clumsy cousin, jerking
on the end of a rope. I am the wet head
hiding in the lily pads, the
crayfish crouched beneath the dock.

Grant can climbswimshootfixdare, any
kind of verb. Grant can. In my dreams
he swings from sumacs while rewiring
toasters and cracking squirrels
on the rocks below. He dives through
my exclamations, my immobile *oh*s.

Nightly I used to dim Grant
in those braggart summer skies.
So what, can he moon or splendour?
When has the world ever needed
someone to run on the water
or rewire the trees?
In the dullest of darks,
I would lose my silhouette
in deep-thought swings and dives.

Older, slightly blurred, life
is not quite so divided. Grant still
swims the bay each morning and
is rumoured to understand the innards
of VCRs. Now it pleases me
to see something bobbing in the waves,
having something explained. Pieces of
Grant. A familiar verb.

In the cut-out past Grant is pasted
over top a paper wave, two pieces
of rope in his capable hands.
I am not in the picture, except for
the merest shadow of a scissor blade.

UNCONDITIONAL LOVE

Undeniable love. Shaking me
by the cuff in a drooling embrace,
wrapping my resistance
in an endless tail. Squirms me
to the rug, a flash of fur,
boy becoming beast, sprouting whiskers
from behind my ear, cold nose
in my cupped palms. Picture
homo sentimentalien and mutt.
Her tongue making territory of my body.

Almost heredity, this doggy love.
Dad and his Airedale
crossing childhood at a trot.
A great uncle and his even Greater Dane
sharing slippers for twenty twilight years.
Cousin Helen with a Pomeranian
grinning from her black patent purse.

Who else but a dog showed me
how to hug, letting my arms go
messy, my kneecaps and navel and chin
all joining in an electric shock?
Who else could make a compliment
out of a bare belly? Canine kisses
taught me true affection, a
stray unselfconsciousness.

Are there dogs in heaven? I asked
my mother, an elastic band
squeezing my heart into
an upstairs/downstairs shape.
No souls, is what she said. A dog
is nothing but an instant, here and
gone. I imagined God
all spine and loneliness, naked
as a bar of soap.

When I go, my dog will go with me.
We'll race past those staunch
pearly gates, to the Happy Hunting
Ground, the Other Side, the Abyss, whatever
it's really called. I'd rather grow
a tail than a pair of stiff wings.
An eternity of unconditional love, that
cold-nosed, no-soul beast.

VISITING NANA

Nana died in 1965, in the middle
of a baseball game, middle of
an adolescent August. *Gone to
glory*, my mother said, just north
of Kingston Road, where the chestnut
trees tower over milky tombstones
and the grass is springy like a Persian
rug. *Selena Mary*, reads the marble
marker, a grasp of geraniums bravely
posing as a flower bed. Eternal 1965:
with Nana, I'm always 13 years old.

Half my childhood moved to St. John's
Cemetery. A grandfather who used to
bounce me on startlingly bony knees.
Aunt Lillian who curled beside me
in her whispering white slip. Uncle Russell
who could make the sidewalks laugh.
And of course Nana, perched in a wheelchair
the clouds have now transformed
into a chariot. *One day*, she promised,
you can be the wind.

I spring across the haunted lawns, each
blade of grass the sliver of a sparrow bone.
Falling chestnuts bump against the statues
of pale angels, heartbeats crack mid-air.
The world bounces through space, clover
fields of stars. Planets smile down
on both the living and the dead.

If Nana were still alive, a furious 122, I'd wheel
her around these nostalgic lawns. 46 myself,
I'd be sure to believe in all sorts and sizes
of loss, doing arithmetic at each tombstone,
reciting weathered epitaphs.
Push me faster, faster, Nana would
complain, years to cover in one short afternoon.

13 or 46, I can take Nana with me wherever
I want. That long-ago moment of my mother
scrubbing the kitchen floor, crying right there
on one clean square of tile. *Tell me again,*
Nana pleads. I explain how tears don't always
fall evenly. Tell her how clover sometimes
makes me think of her long white hair. I smile
at these and other happy stories, a steady breeze.

I leave the cemetery gates empty-hearted,
hollow against the sudden onslaught of years.
Adolescence spread across the parking lot
where I tower over cars, my feet sinking
in the summer asphalt. 13 almost quadruples
itself, time-lapse photography of geraniums
shooting to seed, marble wearing away like skin.

There are so many years from either end
of glory. My mother, too arthritic
to scrub a floor, is almost there.
The child my wife and I never had, still
a sparrow bone, a strand of clover.
Only visiting Nana do I feel my every act
and thought eternal, the wind wheeling
clouds around and around the world.

HOLY FACE

His hands and sleeves held out
like estuaries, reaching for the sea
of me. Jesus looming
from my bedroom wall, dominating
the pirate curtains and kitty
calendar, even the moonlight
that hangs from my closet door. In
the early hours of the morning, His
fingertips inch over hardwood
floors, little drowning pools of light.

Hours alone, just the two of us,
staring. Boldly, I'd pull back the covers
and show Him my bum, something
to shock the nakedness of His baby
fingers, the way the nails
were so translucently pink
I could see the prayers beneath. Fingers
that could wipe away my scars and
moles, polish me to ivory bone,
to deadly essence.

The only one in the house awake, the
only one in the whole of Scarborough, I
knew His holy face would never be calm,
never stop glowing, until I was good and
gone. Such naked love, wanting me
for all eternity. The picture frame, the
wall, the brick beyond, they all
dissolved, the stars grabbing at me
with greedy fingers.

Not until seventeen did I replace that picture
with a poster of Jimi Hendrix
wrestling with a blinding white guitar.
Now Christ could only reach me
with childhood memories, a
giant octopus looming from
a picture-book sea, a world
aeons beyond my Aztec curtains
and lava lamp. An occasional
nightmare: a severed hand
sharing the same white maggot pillow,
or a disembodied finger
lifting my lashes, the light
as bottomless as a tidal wave.

ENDLESS PRAYERS

God save my precious cat
from the crushing teeth of
Mr. Allen's answered prayer
of a Cadillac.
Save her from the cobra
branches of the willow
where the mother wren
is praying for her squiggly young.
Save her from the Doberman
who owns the street
and prays for things he shouldn't.
Save her from the insatiable
fat man on the corner
whose prayers are prayed with
knives and forks.
Save her from ditches and sewers
where the devil only pretends to pray.
Save her from the blue Persian
in next door's basement
who howls nightly
for love and devotion.
Save her from the full moon
where unanswered prayers
go wild.
Save her from that vicious
mouse of death
that only looks and squeals
like a mouse
because it's run out of prayers.

USELESS BOYS

There's an automotive warehouse
in the north end of the city
backing on a field that for
a few weeks every summer
is full of daisies. My father
has his lunch out there. The warehouse,
his twenty-year stint; clocks stretched around
his legs, a paycheque over his
mouth. The years are showing,
responsibilities wrecking
his heart.

Such a moth-life is not for me –
remember how we'd talk? . . . all our
plans were promises not to be
like our fathers. No direction
to go, just a finger of a
man telling us which way not to.
We were going to be free, dashed
away by any wind that came
along. No padlocked love, no tokens.
We said we were afraid of mouse-grey
interiors, of men who limped,
of buildings where they paid you to age.

So how did it go? . . . one of my
arms has turned into a pen. I'm
blind now but there's Braille. I build
a better world on paper
then sell it. Someone told me you
were living in an air
conditioner, just counting the
money. Here's to you. We must have
been crazy. Lucky us, useless
boys, found cures for all our dreams.

KNEE-HIGH

Knee-high to a man whose knees were
too busy banging together
to give me a pony ride.
He was the nervous type,
skittering from Monday to Sunday,
rearing at every rattle of emotion, terrified
at the blot of his own shadow
on the sun-streaked living-room rug.
He was a bone tambourine,
a trembling of rain on tin.

Lick him, stamp him, send my father
through the mail: *Attention*
Manufacturer, this model doesn't work.
How could he snuggle me
when his hands were shaking?
Where was the comfort
when his worst was always worse?
Send me the pop-up dad
with big, steady knees
and a will like a Swiss Army knife.

It was always night when I felt
the connection, hooked
in unholy fear,
my whole body banging,
horrors passed on to me,
havoc in the blood.
There I was, kicking away
the covers, gasping for light.

Wait for me, I'd call
as he scurried from jump to jitter.
I'd run towards him across the yard,
dodging and ducking
as if the sun were a loose chandelier.
Until I realized I was afraid of him,
not the man in the moon
and his burst balloons, not
an avalanche of icy daggers,
not even the dire facts
of growing old and becoming dead.
Afraid of finally climbing
his anxious knees, two shattered ponies,
like riding broken glass.

INCOMPLETE WITHOUT HER

I am the miniature rose she pins to her chest,
the ouch skewering the crossroads of my spine
where my nerves branch into personality traits.
Every time she reaches for her heart
she touches me, tucking in my shirt,
wiping away my face, tugging at
my gravity, my curls. The kisses on my cheek
are her crafty way of making me
look robust, encouraging all my childless aunts
to graze me with powder and perfume.

In private she prepares me for the day
when I'll outgrow her, planting cells
from her voice box in my ears,
grafting peels of her skin on my tongue.
She squeezes her fist up inside of me,
spreading her fingers so I can never forget
how far she was willing to go. Even further,
she switches my nipples like a pair of crossed eyes,
then my testicles, throwing me off-balance
in case of future desire. Finally
she sucks out my soul in one mammoth gulp,
replacing it with a raw, hollow gasp.

She teaches me I am incomplete without her
until God does away with his body counts,
blending each with the other, sons
disappearing into mothers, no such thing
as alone anymore.

SECTION 2

. . . much thought to the scheme of writing: a million words honeycombed in my brain, each for its own perfected purpose, a clear glass bell. How many times have I sat and listened to someone drone on predictably when suddenly they utter a pearl? By God, my eardrums echo and my toes curl. A phrase like *I'm about as beat as the backside of a rug* or *The cat hedge-hopped up to the butter dish*. The blandest face blazes with imagination: a brain like no other, a private compartment on a flying train. There's no reason to be dusty-tongued with a rusty voice box squeezing out squeaks. The world's aloft with all sorts of undiscovered similes and metaphors. Writing is an apple snapping its branch, a wave exploding, the swerve of a kiss . . .

DISAPPEARING GRANDMOTHERS

Nana is the one with the Bible
waving in her mauve hand, eclipsing
a perfect summer's day. Grammie
preferred pocketbooks, *Valley of the
Dolls*, tragedies she could
stuff in an apron pocket.
Sneaking peeks at both made
me equally afraid, all that talk
of sin. Women stripped to salt,
burning up with fevers, ravaged
by darkness, handsome snakes.

Nana, of course, was headed for heaven,
her long white hair tangled
in an angel's toes. But Grammie,
brazen as a magnifying glass,
would be torn to pieces by her lack
of faith, words yanked
off the page and scattered
in countless unhappy endings.

Yet they both died the same, middle-
of-the-night gasps, open windows.
Both bodies heavy as
encyclopedias. Nana's hair twisted
into an anchor. Grammie's glasses
so clean, they weren't really there.

Heaven and hell wore similar expressions,
teeth chewing on the insides of
lips, eyes overwhelmed by lids.
Dead angels or gruesome
dolls. Years later, my mother
was still wearing both their aprons,
her wet hands disappearing into the pockets
like lost souls.

ACCORDION NOTES

Accordion in the hall closet,
hasn't breathed for years. Bellows must be
dusty. I strap it on my shoulders,
let it hang like huge musical breasts,
pass my palms over the keys. The tuning
of a band. My cat keeps her distance.

Accordion gasping in the narrow hall,
keys trembling. Wheezing now, taking
breaths the size of rooms.

I sit on the bare floor, prop my feet
against the wall and dangle my
fingers against the keys.
A rusty "Star Dust" for the mystery
in my cat's eyes. She opens green and wide,
mews at the end of each faltering chorus.

Music hobbles from the fake ivory
and memories of Italian teachers
and recitals of "Whispering Hope"
drift in the hall. I play "Blue Danube Waltz"
for my wife in the shower. I play until
I pass out on the floor and then the accordion
carries on without me, using my heart as a pump
playing polkas and beer songs until dark.

Music triumphs. Cat creeps closer,
smelling bellows and swatting loose straps.
I feel as if I'd learned to walk again.
The night stretches on while the cat and I,
sitting like her male friends on fences,
howl tributes to a pale, melodic moon.

LOVE PLACE

Sopping through candied heart canals,
slithering along the blue banks of the wrist,
rolling in agony on the tongue –
there is no such spot as love.

Better to stretch, spread out:
vertebrae velvet on the lips. Intoxicating
collarbones of sweat. Fingers
one by one exhaled.

Soon love is sighted everywhere,
circulation bold. It cools in
the open lap or lumps together on
the head of a nipple. It graces the pores.

Ah, the multiplicity of love.
The hairs on the back of a palm
bristle, each one a stroke, a
sweetness, a crease on the tongue.

Unpremeditated, shivers form a breast,
a thigh, an ankle. The shape
of love strains and varies.
Forever temporary, offhand.

Tonight, embrace the pancreas in a
shower of insulin, then the earlobe
which was made to fit a space between the teeth.
The buttocks, as always, will be electric.

A moment only for this – your passion,
your other planet, your sex – whatever
the air forms. Hold it in your arms
and feel the breath escape . . . that's love.

The isolated organ is a microscopic slide.
A moment merely a biopsy of the senses.
An orgasm breaks the webbed bones
and runs the gamut of nervy hollowness.

Love shoots the system and fools it whole.

PICTURE DESIRE

A kiss, the moon rushed off its feet,
a toppled bedroom lamp.
How desire is announced,
lips like a purple marquee,
a bruising of ecstasy.
Deep and squeezed, that slippery pose,
shadows dipped between your breasts.

All I really want to do
is be with you, a rendezvous . . .
you sigh and say your heart
is just a little lower down.

Such sweet pieces of ourselves.
Black stockings wrapped around
your ankles, my shirt-tail stuck
in a crease, the room haphazard
with mismatched shoes, discarded pants
and pillows flattened against the walls.

You call me your lover
or else, the man who fit
amazing parts of himself
into your favourite fantasy.
I respond with the shape of you
on my mouth, a purple word.

Dwelling in the dark recesses
of blurred desire,
no one can tell where either
one of us begins.
Whose shadowy arms, whose
mid-air moon?

All I really want to do
is reach beyond my need
for you, a hand daring
a dark room. This is what
I want, that deep chill where
every piece of me is given up.

SINGING

We file in, filling the pews
with sensible shoes. A sniff of
understated lilac perfume.
Fingertips pooling on Bibles.
The organ murmuring like the
wires in a long-distance call.

Sunday droops in its crystal vase.
This hollow church – a crack of knees
sounds deep within the wooden walls.
Stained-glass angels hide behind their
purple wings. The priest whispers things
to his wide white robe. Holy, all
as one . . . holy, the swallowed tongue.

Prayer and blessings, the voice box
tingling at the mention of love.
A reading from the Book of Luke
politely clears the throat. Soon
a sermon lilting in our ears.

Listen up, listen here, repeat
the loudness of the Lord. We
are learning how to speak in
metaphors. How to creak and roar.

Hymns, tuneless, dive from bottom lips.
Shakespeare on a binge, Cole Porter
with a limp, the words and music
rising in us. All those
trembling adjectives, haunting verbs.
Christ cracked as a high note, held.

When I sing I am not so
sensible. The soul, a bold
and noisy place. Week to week
Sunday's simple face looks up,
speaks out. No doubt the sound is
awful to the disinclined:
the twisted larynx of a saint.

But how we try, explain, express,
the hugeness of it all. Singing
to a silent God, a swallowed
faith. Singing out that ancient dream.

FEELING THE HEAT . . .
CEYLON 1922

May my eulogy advise that
once upon a time I survived
that scalding island known as
Ceylon. *In 1922*
the less-than-honourable
Mr. Lawrence almost died
from devilish heat, from shock.

Frieda shrugs both shoulders bare
her face protruding in the
snapping sun. *Pick me a coconut,*
she sings. How the wife has a taste
for the poison in her husband's brain.
Her words take aim and flare.

I dream of her dancing over
steamy hills, the Lake of Kandy
coarse in the distance. A dance of
tea and cinnamon, of pealed
temple bells. Naked as
a Buddha, a real bellyful.

She dances night and day, six weeks
of footsteps in my memory.
These tropics are a selfish place:
stoking women into sparks
burying their men beneath
boiling rubber. Where loneliness sweats.

In my last dream Frieda is
a rather large flower, lazy
scarlet with petals loose as
tongues. And I, a worker bee
drowning in hot nectar
a final, choking buzz.

May Ceylon mistake the ocean
for a flower (and bending
to the scent, sink amidst
the scarlet waves). I am taking
Frieda out of dreams, my fist rising
on a cool pen. Passion
is better made than endured.

THE GOD POEMS

1. *Sand*

> At first sign of God
> I'll wear a tattered
> T-shirt, gravedigger's
> boots, a shovel raised
> in my hands like a
>
> prayer. Let the tomb and
> feet blur together,
> down deep as if upon
> my knees, facing up
> to my own mortality.
>
> Surrender, a trick
> of calculated
> innocence. Spiders
> and ants can't eat me,
> not if I detect
>
> them first. Listen to
> the music of nails,
> the high-pitched whine of
> wood, the drumbeat rap
> of earth, that toy house
>
> of my father crumbling.
> God creates other
> signs. Age, bloody rocks,
> a star with a message.
> Says I'm made of mud.
>
> *Walk with Me through*
> *waterlogged roses,*
> *brush against cold, cold*
> *stone.* How delicate
> all the life is, the

beating-heart Bibles,
the unsteadiness
of houselights, like
angels. I dig deep
decapitating

roses, drowning sand
with sand, wary of
the back-broken rocks,
the soft knock of grass,
the roots entangled

in the fair, familiar
skin. The tricks with strings
of sand, a cat's
cradle of Holy
Ghosts. I will not heed

a final sign, a
landslide, or clouds
accompanied by
hooks. Let Him drag a
river for me, burn

down a closet, hire
a detective. I
live, shaking sand out
of my pockets by
the shovelful.

2. *Trying to Rearrange the Sky*

The sky is full of
possibilities,
ladders, rearrangements
of tall angels, a
sneaking of ropes. Come

each morning, the bright
yellow sky crowds with
paraphernalia
the dead cling to but
always leave behind.

The clouds are fresh flowers.
The hint of stars, soft
footsteps mourning the
grass. And the wind, which
begins in space, turns

all heartbeats down again,
the earth trembling as
if with the sounds of
falling bodies. Such
threats in the sky. God

glaring, a brassy
sun, big-shot airplanes,
teasing birds, endless
beauty as the years
fade more quickly and

your feet ease off the
ground. Enough. Say it,
shout it, words might
disfigure the fear.
Rearrangements,

exchange the trees for
the stars, the earth for
emptiness. In spite
of our lives we will
stand on our heads.

3. *God's Own Voice*

And in the beginning
there was sand and sky,
a choice of men or
cloud. Trees pointing high
or squatting round like

an embrace. Skin to
place over your own
skin when night narrowed
in like a snake. And
there was guilt, dreams of

flight, the wide awake
greed for gravity,
the desire and
the far-flung denial.
Still you thought you could

escape Me, when? . . . Did
the candles burn out,
did the dark make you
giddy, were your bodies
as light as imagination?

And in the middle
there was consternation,
birds bled from the wind,
bellies tingling and
sinking low, children

bred like castles in
the sand. And the trees
died standing up, and
the people rearranged
themselves like clouds.

The world became round,
standing on the print
of a thumb. No talk
of miracles. Just
change. Bodies aged to

sand. All life turned upside
down and believed in
once again. And in
the end, nothing contrived,
no one to console.

Life is sand and sky
or nothing at all.
I am consistent
in every way,
careful, concise.

The number of heads that
can fit on the flat
of a shovel? I
know. This endless prairie
life. I hear. Your foot-

steps echo in the
sand. Believe. The sky
grows dark and absent
like a man who chooses
to grieve alone.

DROWNING

There are people weeping into
Bibles, smudging the print, crying
because Jesus fades. They're sitting
on the edge of the world as
if it were a bed, shoes half-off,
dangling into space. There is
no faith left, no barefoot place in
their hearts. Rooms are grey, like nests,
pages thick with twigs and mud. They
sit, half-blind Bibles sopping wet,
little children welling over
in their eyes. The children are
perfect copies of themselves
before their crying.

He talks to some of them, wades in
their tears, says things about light, dry
spells, how together they could soak
up oceans. Their eyes flicker, the
kids fidgeting, so quick to
believe. Their Bibles fall, go
under. They open their mouths to
speak. Words held back by angels,
angels as dry as sun.

I lie on my back, drifting, most
of my body submerged. There are
no islands. I watch the clouds, the
shapes they take, what life was once,
before all the water. People
tell me the tops of trees
separate us from sky. They say
it's in the Bible. But when I
look, all the words have been wept
away. On the shiny blank pages
I see my own reflection.

THE SEARCH

I have searched under stones
for signs of hope, all that buoyant bug life.
Stared at the eyelids of sleeping friends,
hoping to catch a glimpse of generosity.
I have held the hearts of Mom and Dad
in my hands, the steady *bump, bump,*
bump of bona fide love.

I have drunk my milk and brushed my teeth,
checked both back and front door locks.
And in the mornings, the windows thick with breath
(wisps of ghosts and wolves), I have whistled
a silent exclamation, one tiny *o*.

*

Caught in the failure of the moment,
I see myself in every chair around the empty table,
each face looking through its fingers,
space divided into walls. I try to lose
myself in dusting and sweeping,
but my own breath keeps filling my lungs
with what might have once been grace.

Absence, the house hollowed of everything
but superstition, desperation, maybe even awe.

*

Dear God, forgive me my grey afternoons.
Bless the wolves fogging up my windowpanes.
This is my flesh and grope.

God whose eyes are closed
and evermore shall only be called eyelids.
Who wears blisters and blood stains,
yet still expects to be part of an orderly house.
Snags a loose bit of brain,
unravels me like a lopsided sweater.

God renowned for his remarkable love,
his power, his vision, his lack of presence.

*

Heavens, where is the hope?
Father bumping into mother who then bumps
into me, all of us entangled in the most generous
of wills. Open the windows, curtains swing
like hot-air ghosts. Search the sky
for all those sky things: cloud shapes, wisps of
moon, sudden gusts of birds. Come sunrise,
I'll crouch neatly under a rainbow,
its strings of coloured water creating a temporary shrine.

HOLDING FATHER

He walks through a grove of crabapple trees,
slipping on and squashing the hard wine fruit.
Younger, he was a rake, curiously clawed.
Now, flat and clumsy, he breaks no ground.

Some apples still hang from wormy branches,
gnawed and puffy from the rain.
The world is no longer smooth, he claims,
but burst into slivers. Someday soon, snap,
the world will dangle, an old man clinging to a leaf.

The interval between stem and bark
is a laboured breath. Thumbs press,
lost in colourless sap.
My father plucks a crab which mushes
in his hand, wipes it on the twisted trunk.
Nothing worse than rotting summer.
Dead apples shining on a sticky branch.

Strange, the clinging. The sickly grove.
He latches on to the farmer's fence,
solid in its snaky curves.
A house can go forever,
this fence, a patio, even chairs.
A careful life contrives to simply outlast.

The orchard road is bold and dry.
Walk with me, a step, request,
walk and turn and climb.
He holds an apple in his hand,
a frail crab, good luck.
Whole it sits on his fingers like a living thing.

2.

Memory is a treasure hunt
through conversations, closets,
layers of skin.

Lawrence Welk and his bubbly *oompah*
bring back slender dances
on the rec-room floor.

The peerage of war vets and lawn mowers,
of garage mechanics and *Look* magazines.
I can't picture him a younger man;
he can't remember the kernel of proof.

Po-faced, he has come to surrender:
his blue wedding suit,
his two-fingered whistle, his hair.
Me with my aching legs, his pacing.
Both of our shouts.
He forgets what his own father looked like,
runs to the photo album on the sly.
Wait until, he's fond of saying –
til memory is a giant rock,
the hands no longer made of TNT.
Where is the pin from Texaco?
What was 1943?

Memory is a caved-in property.
The shock of forgetting yourself.

3.

The years collapse, a manslide.
Head over heart, will never stop.

A little boy flies by my father's window,
a comforting squeal, sweeping gone.
The world is raining boys of all ages,
a boast of thunder. Catch their eyes,
they are filled with the wonder of their fall.

Cousins in the treetops,
giant uncles peering from streetlamps.
That birdy teacher appears
in a cloud of coloured chalk.
The first boss, booming plentiful.
Blind dates with fingers
twirling in their hair.

A young man: Dear, Teddy, Mister.
Everyone is calling for my father,
wants and schemes,
a drift of August in the air.
Opening his first Texaco:
gasoline dreams of suburban flowerbeds.
Marrying, a colour scheme,
a kiss the length of a bed.
A son, perfect to the frequent touch.

The casual years fall slow-motion.
He is almost an eagle,
the delicious suddenness of swoops.
The house floats, the wife breezes,
the baby boy unclouds his eyes.

A middle-aged man stones by the window,
landing on a service-station floor.
Money dies on trees,
rainbows stinking in the gasoline.
My father leaps on life, no sucker,
but life collapses underneath.
Ulcers, anger, the downwind hooks it all.

Fat cats, explorers, golden boys,
my father sheds personas in the beating rain.
Finally retires, a pin.
The window smokes, yet still the sound
of old men zooming by.
Time is a blur in the middle of the room;
did it happen, will it, which?

Lately my father sees bones
dropping from the sky,
strives to scare us.
Yep, saw a ghost, saw that bugger Death.
This world is nothing but a trampoline
and life's the fall.
Better to see these crazy things than be.
Look, a funny bone tumbling fast.

4.

On the golf course, knocking
the rubber out of that ball.
My father bends and glares, swinging his hips.
Eyes the sun as if he'd launched an Icarus.
Did you see that? he calls, his grassy brag.
He can still knock hell off the beam.
Seventy-two and doing.

Lying in his lap, a kid,
his hands buried most of me.
Little chip. Little man.
Throw me, Dad, the wind severe,
the sky blooming.
The game of serious life.

My father follows the flight
of each and every ball,
his club swooning to the green.
The way he used to look at me,

bouncing from his arms,
a confidence more precious than love.
A follow-through.

I mispronounce his longings, I tower over him,
I want to beat his ball,
but on the fairway, stormy, tired,
I follow his every move. Memorize.
This is what my father looks like
knocking the stuffing from a golf ball . . .
burned on all my eyes.

The swing, the pride. I can feel him
in my hands. A shot of sun.

5.

Hugging another man, I feel myself:
ribs, sighs, sticky palms.
I walk into my father's arms afraid.

A blush, a bruise. Still solid, severe.
Standing his own ground,
not knowing when to close his eyes.

This is not a request for affection.
Nothing to reassure. This is a leap
from a windowsill, my father watching me fly.

We forget for a moment and bump,
good old male love.
There are handshakes in our timid hearts.

Stepping in, I throw myself around him,
tripped toes, a squeeze. His shoulder blades
almost collapse. We breathe.

His arms go up, a swoop.
He holds me for an instant,
a piece of the vast and falling sky.

BLEEDING HEARTS

While orange lilies peeled off
their bikini straps
and roses did the mambo,
the bleeding hearts just hung their heads
and bled.
No interlude between life and death,
not for these martyrs
dripping from their stems
like unbearable drops of sweat.
Makes me think of faith,
Nana said,
a dark bouquet
wilting her wrist.

All summer long
the garden exposed itself,
bruises and testicles,
gallstones and moles.

While the lilies stripped
and the roses danced their way
to hell,
the bleeding hearts died
over and over again
as everyone in Scarborough
would eventually die,
falling towards the dust
in the middle of a deep pink blush,
embarrassed
at having lived at all.

SWALLOWED SONG

I swallow you: a snake transfigured
by the shape of its hunger.

Adam with a huge love
caught in his throat.

The tongue is connected to a heart,
a groin; kisses bonding the intimate
body. Acrobatic muscles, hollow bones.

Together, we are placeless. Elusive
possibilities. The best I can do
is bleed you a map on my skin:
blushing, bruised. The body spent and shared.

Love does not discriminate between
a lip and a nipple. In love, both are
pigments of the whole skin. No proof
exists but hunger: each devouring, disappeared.

My mouth contains you, one stray cell
sucked from the softness of your neck.
Look, love is one nakedness
made from more than enough.
That blushing shape is not misplaced;
is always there, like a huge tattoo.

There, we swallow, *ah*. We are
swallowed by the long night, the snaky
bed. Forever hungry for the shape of
each other, our gulping hands.

Come, love is connected to love, to
anything claimed in the name of love.
A kiss, a muscle.
The heartbeats all over the body,
pulse points transfiguring.

This is all a love song.
From the blood. Elusive body . . .

I am a lip, you a nipple.
The snake swallows; connected,
contained, we are devoured whole.

THE BROKEN MAN

I plant my broken self
in the garden. Earth will secure
my cracked chambers, rain soothe
my sorry scars. Longing for
sunlight to raise the dead.

The colour green swells everywhere
while all my strength can manage
is a pale hope. I am the wilted
stem breaking through the seed.

Think of such a garden,
some stolid marigolds, a haughty
rose bush here and there,
an inconspicuous man crouched
among the violets. How flowers
steal a sorrow's edge.

A bud is a pang of love,
love a tiny drop of blood
squeezed painfully from the heart.

Rejuvenation, the garden pulsing
with July, a body with roots.
Come autumn, that cruel harvesting
of comfort, blossoms will be buried
beneath treefuls of leaves. I wish
I could be saved as something
dried and lovely in a winter vase.
Splendidly inhuman.

Instead, I will walk out of
the earth, yet another Adam
healed for a season or two,
and on cold, cold nights
I will be listening to
the frozen petals of violets
as they exhale tiny cries of pain.

THE DEAD ARE WATCHING US

The dead are watching us . . . grandfathers,
great-aunts with faces yellow as bungalow bricks,

distant pioneers administering desire in long
lingering looks, their stone-cold irises enthralled.

They are in love with the sleek black carpets
of our driveways, the bundles of rhubarb

soaking in stainless steel sinks, the tiny rubber skiffs
floating pink ovals of soap across our steamy tubs.

They are longing for luxury, for contentment,
those hammocks stretched between elms

and telephone poles, those toffee-coloured Buicks
purling at the curbs like Burmese cats,

those silver-threaded clotheslines spinning
with lusty sheets. They are green as cut stems,

as bleeding grass, with envy.

What would they give to sink their bones
in our broadloom, to squeeze their hands

down our elastic waistbands, to collapse on
our porcelain thrones? Eternity

for the blue pulse of a TV set, the chill
of a dinner bell, the creak of a back fence

as it divides us into conversations and families.
They would lie or steal for the opportunity

of sleeping next to us, cotton bums as soft
as lettuce leaves, nipples the size of rosebuds.

They would kill us for our silverware, our cameras,
our Christmas tree angels, those assets

proving we're alive, the crystal butter dish,
the walnut pipe, the painting of a long-haired Christ

whose eyes are blessing everything he sees.
The dead detest us for all of it, our accordions,

our clothespins, our bowls of red-hot porridge.
They can't wait for us to retire from

this luck, a gruesome heart attack or snivelling
cancer cell. Once we've recovered from the thrill

of our souls floating over the Scarborough Bluffs,
we will know exactly what it's like to watch

how much we've left behind.

SECTION 3

THE BLUFFS

1.

The dirty blue of danger
where smelts beach themselves
in mass suicides, where avalanches
land, where disobedient children drown . . .

2.

Walking along the sand,
a mere boy, toenails caked
with clay, his T-shirt
wrapped around his head
like Aladdin's turban.
In nearby bushes
a possible pervert lurks,
all set to pounce.

Or else . . . the boy will be shot
by spy boats from Buffalo, or
catch gangrene from that couple
fucking behind a petrified log.
There's always the chance of
a lost shark snapping up the surf
or Armageddon with its tidal waves.
Maybe even tornadoes, earthquakes, UFOs.

Don't go near those Bluffs,
his mother begs, tying her fingers
into hopeless knots. Down the centuries
a zillion little boys have disappeared,
beaches blonde with drifting bones.
Lake Ontario is nothing but
a giant dish of poison,
the Pied Piper rising from the guck
and steam, his body dripping rats.

3.

Inside, the Bluffs are miles and
miles of bridges, none of which
ever touch the ground. Above
and around, stars glitter like
mole's eyes, nothing left unseen.
It's the dead who ride these
catwalks, these flying tracks,
ride them for the shock of speed.
He imagines himself soaring non-stop,
part of the same intoxicating blur.
Going nowhere has never felt so
necessary, so vital.

4.

He dreams himself into a ball
on the edge of the Bluffs and
tumbles, twirling through burrs
and thistles, bouncing into thin air
and back, somersaulting down
slopes of clay, hitting the beach
like a boulder, free-wheeling
into the spiralling waves.
He floats all the way to Buffalo,
that motherless, dangerous land.

5.

Abducted, the ramifications of such
a daring word. He pictures himself
striding down the beach
on a hot summer's day, everything
forbidden luxuriating in his veins.
Suddenly, a flurry, the breeze
scattering, a raven's wing strong
as a shovel, scooping him up and away.

Down, down below, mothers dangle
from clotheslines, their apron pockets
filled with stones. The streets
completely empty of children,
hopscotch squares fading
by the minute.

If only the Bluffs were equipped
with an engine, he would drive them
into the wild blue distance.
The lake captures such a fine reflection
of the cliffs, he often thinks of
submarines, those peaks and pinnacles
like periscopes aimed at the moon.
If only the Bluffs were a Saturday morning
cartoon that could simply stomp away,
shaking off the tiny, perfect houses,
toppling hedges and garden gates,
all the mothers tangled in one another
as they roll into the hungry waves.

HORSES THAT COULD FLY

Metamorphosis of night
on moving brain – the white horse moon
cascading over fields,
the yellow eyes of stars.

A man with matches flaring in his fists
chases the disappearing clouds,
reason fleeing. Darkness falls
like dusty curtains, birds flying
in their sleep, blood tumbling
in the light of body, in
the star-lined horse and eye.

Mother sits beside me, reading
about horses that could fly.
About blind men with tongues on the tips
of their fingers. Little energies
jolting fairy tales to life:
kidnapped, rewritten, astounded,
eaten alive. The moon spills
from a crayon box. The bumpy
inspiration of wild boys,
midnight limits exploded,
silver skies with scrawled orange comets.

Think, on the back of a horse,
of falling, of too thin-moon,
Persian eyes bearing through pillows,
God and his invisible chimes.
Metamorphosis of
fear to trust, of legs to manes,
of light to moving brain, of
horses in the picture book
to horses thundering in
the wide awake, dark-inspired sky.

Anticipating sleep, a trot
around the room on hoof-like heels,
the giddiness of imbalance. Eyes
closed, ten minutes steeped in story,
the horse soars to Africa
and back, nose to nose with God,
totally confident of
its imaginary wings.

Think of all the boys falling
into the impossible. Think
of creatures with steaming eyes
and smoking manes, of flames searing
across the sky, escaping logic.
As the world sleeps and watches,
let the horses leap
until they run out of light.

SEASONS

1.

I claim there is trust, room
enough in the heart
for buds and corn, for cold
trees, useless fields of frost.

Your heart is small though,
a drift of snow in the corner
of a blurred backyard.

Eyes, no matter what their colour,
see the same. We both watch
birds wheeling south, black
shadows on the endless streets.

Are we willing to believe
in shapes, in patterns?

Lie down beside me,
the sky is soft, open now.
If suddenly a stray feather
revolves upon your wrist,
think of one heartbeat,
how without you, who knows,
it might fall forever.

2.

Perhaps trust is a pilgrimage
to the bottom of your heart.
Roots remain with trees
in bitter frosts, a pulse
in an unconscious body.

Warm then, warm, no matter
when, there are birds connected
to the land through our eyes.

Birds falling to eternal
July, south of doubt, in spite
of tiny hearts that often
freeze, mid-flight, an ice cube
poised before an open mouth.

Come, a drift of you,
a promise patient
in my frozen hands.

Our hearts ache, a tight prism
of fist, reflected light,
a field of snow beginning
to blossom in the sky.

SWINGING INTO SPACE

Only twelve years old, thrashed by leukemia,
an inhuman word like *amputee* or
gruel. The creak of schoolyard
swings, a wind playing all alone.
The hurt colours of collapsed
tulips. None of us had ever
lived through such a ruthless spring
before. The last breaths of
puddles soaking through the canvas
of our running shoes.

Our Sunday school teacher claimed
suffering was less than it seemed,
meaning all we could do was accept.
God knows best, a magician dematerializing
a rabbit. No one ever returned
from the dead though, not even Houdini,
let alone a twelve-year-old girl. Creak,
creak, an empty swing flying
off the Scarborough Bluffs, creating
more and more space.

At the end, her voice was a
whimper, a penny dropped over
Niagara Falls. As if someone was
pinching her elbow, shutting her up.
And so, we never listened. A
muffled dying, like being lost
inside a rock.
All we could do was ache, our
grandmothers' rheumatism warping
our thoughts. Discovering
a centipede's pain, leg by leg
plucked off. Butterflies with
wings torn in two. Robin's eggs
smashed. Learning that our bodies
could turn to leukemia
in seconds flat.

When she died, she only took
a little of herself with her, leaving
all that empty space for us. No matter
how hard we tried to imagine, heaven
was no bigger than a pebble or a bud.
It was the world swinging in the
wind, the world collapsing, the
world gasping for breath.

How we longed for those thin layers
of early spring ice, something between
us and pain. A line to leap across, to
slide over. A window
limiting fate to a glance.

BELIEVING IN BILLY

Hong Kong, Sydney, New York, amongst
thousands of uplifted faces
a man stands on stage
beneath dreamy lights.

Microphone in his mouth,
bellowed psalms. Proverbs in
universal tongues.

His hands hold tight
a gleaming Bible, the world
smoothed, compressed like coal.

Are those angels in his eyes
blue with hope, squeezed small as stones?

He is world-loved, held precious
in a TV camera's boxy arms.

The Ladies Home Journal
declares him holier
than Christ. My mother, light-swept
in her soggy chair, swears
he is equal to John the Baptist.

Billy, when you swallow
at the end of prayer,
are you talking to God?

Will you raise your arms
outstretched for just a moment?

Can you touch me, hand to
shoulder, a swooning dance?

Might you save a man
from choking on himself?

Your head is bowing through
my TV set, your hair streaked white
a halo tilted with the years.

I like to watch your hands
steadying the crowds,
a man with perfect posture.

And your eyes, I love to see
them drop into the Bible,
angels falling to their knees.

But TV always ends, living
rooms dry as plaster, the world
dark and fabric once again.

Where do you go, Billy?
You are a lot like God –
a flickering glimpse.

The TV set grows cold and
safe, the site of an ancient
miracle. A long-lost heaven
of makeup and dreamy lights.

This night, a tongue-tied
prayer. Something to sustain
me, a microphone.

That same old prayer – can you see me,
see me . . . is anybody there?

GIVING BIRTH

I wouldn't want to have given birth
to Christ, she said. And I imagined
the fierceness of angels, the will of
wind, an embryo eating up
all the hope and desire in her body,
the lungs, the liver, even the
electric gristle of nerves and
bones, swallowing all the traces
of herself, the darkest secrets,
the shivers, leaving behind an emptiness
incandescent as a meteor.

It was bad enough giving birth
to you, she said, something in her eyes
doubling over, clutching itself.

Gathered round his worn-out sandals,
their sense of selves impetuous and
slight, they felt their shadows shrinking
like the punchlines of parables.
Most of them were obedient enough
to plunge headfirst through a needle's
eye, willing to bleed their drops of
Welch's Grape, to change their last names
to Christ. They aimed for flawlessness,
nails hammered straight, the colour flesh
never straying into the colour red.
Imagine the concentration, a buzzing circle
of six-year-olds, squeezing their dreams
a thousand years old. Little girls
hearing echoes belly-deep, their
names being called and called. Boys
feeling their hearts slamming against
the walls of their chests. Until
their shadows grew too small, a grain of
sand apiece. Until their souls
blossomed like beads of sweat.

GOING TO HELL

Going to hell, easy as
going downstairs,
that gruesome rec room
where the devil spins
on a chrome bar stool
wasting away, watching
late-night TV, or cheating
at a solitary game of darts.

Walking the streets
on drizzly October nights
I can see all the fathers
framed in their basement windows,
frenzied over blades and drills,
a mix of sawdust and sweat
the colour of dried blood.

Or on hazy summer mornings
waking up to find our mothers
gone, washing machines moaning
in laundry rooms, ironing boards
dressed in starched white shirts
like corpses. Creeping down,
down, they appear in billowing clouds
of steam, wringing the bleach
from their wrists and elbows,
struggling for a purity they can't quite
see, even the light bulbs smothered in fog.

*

Going downstairs . . .
the bogeyman behind
the furnace, the tarantula
in the potato bin, the killer
turd in the kitty litter box.

How much does it cost
to go to hell? Just a thought,
the thought you never want
to think, but can't
get out of your head.

Years pass, my spine
transformed into a flight
of cellar stairs. Here
are my fingers huddled
in the corner, mindlessly
playing with themselves.
The rest of me wrapped
around joists and beams, brains
hanging from exposed wires,
body parts buried in cement.

*

Going to hell is a daily trip,
step by step, worry by
worry, losing myself in the sickly
sweet fumes of ant traps,
dust balls suffocating silverfish,
spiderwebs smearing windowpanes . . .
the clinging terrors of everyday death.

MARY SPEAKS TO JESUS

You came from the east
like the sun. I was bending
over a well, pulling up a full
bucket, facing you, not knowing,
the light, your light, spilling
over my face. There was an
explosion in my belly, my bucket
splashing down into the well.

You sprang from me on a cold night.
Your tiny bloody body steamed as if
it had come from a fire and your
hot mouth melted the ice from my breasts.
The earth turned green again as you
grew. Things changed with you. My
milk dried, you never wept like other
babies. I'd lay you under the sky, half-
expecting you to turn into a bird,
half-wanting it.

Everyone recognized you as a child,
even though most would never admit.
They'd look at me, eyes cast down,
thoughts gleaming on the ground before
my feet. They thought you were an angel,
not trusting you, a pink little boy, too
alive to know so much about the deaths
inside of them. How you put shows on for
all those people, quiet dramas, head
tilted up to heaven, pudgy hands open,
palms up, as if you were balancing God.

Looking at you, I could see the future.
It was hard loving you,
seeing the scars on your feet before
you could even walk, stopping myself from
constantly wiping away blood.
Forgive me. When I heard you'd rolled away
the tombstone, I couldn't help wishing
you'd rolled it down into the city,
sun setting, caving in the crowds.

GREEN AS THE VEIN IN
A YOUNG MAN'S DESIRE . . .

EASTWOOD, 1906

Green as a leaf's vein. Green as
a thumbprint in moss. Green
as confetti on stillborn ponds
as infant grass.
Asleep in a meadow
my bare chest stains green.
The nestled loin stone
the polished jade.

Somehow the forest overwhelms
most of life. Chestnut roots
crack kitchen floors, holly leaves
scratch downstairs doors, rabbits
eat entire dresser drawers.
I dive from my gaping bedroom window
and am instantly stripped and shrunk.

The mines grow arthritic, blacken
back to dirt and undergrowth. The town
squats on its squalid hill and strains.
In the moonlight a young man
runs tiny in the valley; a darting
nakedness, escape. In a bed
of violets, an exhausted embrace.

Women here turn red as berries
their slippers sinking in the leaves.
Shopgirl smiles whisked aside, strands
of scented hair. Bare ankles
marvellous in blue brooks. I would like
nothing better than to bleed
those berries between my fingertips.

Such are the tripping fantasies
of an Eastwood lad with the woods
set free in his nerves and wrists.
If only the world were totally green.
Men walking entire countries
with nothing hidden, blossoms
bursting in their eyes, each glance
a colour, a bouquet of flesh.

Green as the vein in a young man's
desire. May all the lovers in the world
be smudged with fingerprints.
The forest thrives through my
bedroom window and carries me away.
Even my nipples are hard as jade.
The world sharpened to a blade of grass.

THE SUNOCO BEAR

On the front lot of the local Sunoco
a grizzly bear surrenders to the rusted bars
of a circus cage, a billboard proclaiming
Put a Growl in Your Gas Tank, King of the Road.
As promised, he growls twelve hours a day,
growls at the ping of the gas-pump bell,
at the chaos of children's shrieks.
The asphalt beneath him rumbles,
the thudding of his giant paws.
Scarborough has never looked so small before,
a shamble, a shuffle, a huge head
smashed against the narrowness of empty spaces.
Set free, he'd tear apart those gawking cars.

At night, the bear light years of blocks away,
my Persian cat pretends to be wild,
leaping from sewing machine to desk,
dodging the shadows of venetian blinds,
sailing over the bottomless toilet bowl,
crash-landing across my ribs.
Let me out, she meows, claws creeping
from her camouflage of softness.

Who isn't trapped? I say,
holding her by the tail.
Look at Nana and her steel canes,
parents and their stingy clocks.
Listen deep down in my chest,
my heart an amateur growl.
The whole of Scarborough grumbles and snarls.

Still the sun rises again and again.
The bear continues to be exploited
for its mixed metaphors.
My cat's wildness succumbs to the summer heat,
a lesser quest for shade and water bowl.
While I forget everything in a game of Kick the Can,
the chant of freedom
clattering up and down the routine street.

REAL LIFE

The only living things left out
on a chilly Scarborough night
are yapping dogs and teenaged boys.
Emptiness with its shadows
crammed in denim pockets, the devil
tugging at his leash. Street lights
overexposing lawns and hedges
a sickly shade of mauve. Such glare,
anything is possible.

He props his mouth open
with a cigarette
and leans against a parked car,
staring through crabapple trees
and bungalows, the aimless aggression
of a dog's constant bark. He feels
like releasing all the yapping Fidos
in this cramped little world. Breathing
so deeply he inhales himself, a mere
phantom mingling with wisps of
chimney soot, another mauve light
undressing the mystery of suburban
darkness, gleaming on the upturned
tails of fleeing dogs.

The stars are pulsing
like proof of eternal life.
The moon wears a barred window
across its creased face, a distant
unfriendly neighbour. He is outside
on his own, waiting for a fantasy,
a teenaged girl wrapped in
a dark red sweater, her arms embracing
the October smoke. The fatefulness
of love is all he can imagine, her arms
gathering him in a naked cloud.

He closes his eyes and the night
is inside him, an extra chamber
for his heart, a newly discovered
thought. Scarborough is just
a convenience, a place to sleep,
a playing-it-safe state of mind.
The same with sunshine
and springtime and all those other
comforts. They give him gravity,
they give him the opposite of
nothingness. Miles and miles
inside him, the night steers
its curves and climbs.

His eyes stay closed long enough
for Scarborough to drift away, unnecessary.
The parked car evaporates
and he is floating in something so silver
it can barely be contained by air.
The fantasy girl is mingling with him,
the colour nude streaming through
his smoky fingers. He imagines
the silky parts of her lips as blue,
daylight reinvented. Their bodies rise,
a pink entanglement, his tongue lost
between her breasts.

When he opens his eyes again
the night is still full of itself, its
convict moon, its sickly street lights.
Everything in place,
except for the colours, and of course
the phantom girl who will one day
be replaced by a real girl
lying in the back seat of a parked car,

her legs spread black and white.
For now Scarborough is one yelp
of disappointment, the boy cramming
his hands so deep into his pockets
he almost squashes his balls.
He would rather be homeless, rather be
free, damn the darkness, that hole in himself
where his soul is supposed to be.

A BIRD IN THE HOUSE

Back door flung open, one of those
same summer days, except for that
single brown breeze, a bird
bouncing off the yellow kitchen walls.

Like hope, he tried everything, wings scraping
against the ceiling, twig feet pinging
in the stainless steel sink, an awful
music, something brittle stuck in the throat.
He flew into the mirror, all self-
destruction, his beak like a shard of glass.

My mother, panic loosening her grip
on faith, began worrying someone would die.
Each feathery crunch another bad luck
blow, a shovelful of superstition.

Only I was calm enough to recognize
one in a variety of God's images.
The stove loomed in the corner like an altar,
the fridge beaming cold white rays of single-mindedness.

With a flick of my wrists, I hid this piece of God
inside a fuzzy tea towel, wrapping him into
a bundle of shivers so soft they were less
than blinks. When I threw him back to the sky
the towel flew higher for an instant, a bird
dropping from it like a magician's hand.

HOW I SURRENDER TO THE DEVIL

The famously crimson glow fills my living room,
a backdrop of red-pepper flames. Wall to wall,
crimson ribs, crimson rugs, the potted plants
smoking, Chagall prints bleeding, lamps like explosions
in miniature action films. How careless I look
in all this flicker, the Devil and I
exchanging handshakes like hunks of raw steak.

A palette apart from golden shimmers of goodness
where even spiders go down on their tiny knees.
Tonight, God sleeps somewhere secret, like a celebrity.
It's just me and the horned one, red and redder,
two roses rubbing up against each other's thorns.
You can smell the envy and lust in the air.
You can look into the sizzle of his eyes
and recognize the grimace on my shrunken face.

We argue for awhile, both of us completely wrong.
We throw ourselves into scalding pits of hate.
Have never felt this free before, flying
into fury and smashing all the shadows on the wall.
Stripped of everything but his steaming socks,
Devil does a lurid dance, the Chagall goats
falling from the sky half-roasted. I throw my head back,
swallowing a snake plant whole. *Party hearty!*
one of us shouts, bursting into a karaoke
version of "Hallelujah Chorus."

Imagine how I feel in the morning,
a field of poppies popping my eyeballs.
Tippy-toeing like a two-year-old, I toddle
towards a trickle of sunlight, hoping
for an unconscious blessing. Hell, what a mess.
The rugs and lamps are still fuming, a pair of
underpants skewered on an aloe vera plant.
How do I make up for this? *Unworthy*, is all
I can manage to say, the tip of my tongue a blister.

The next time I see God, I'm going to wave harder
than all the other fans, make angel eyes at him,
maybe even toss him a flower, something white
like a suffering child's hand. Who knows,
maybe he'll hire me as a houseboy
to carry guests' coats or fetch pretty snacks
from his yellow kitchen.
Maybe I can even learn to turn the Devil down
before he whispers his inklings in my ear,
flee through those alluring clouds of smoke.

CAPRICORN

Down the cellar steps, behind the furnace,
sits a scuffed black telescope
filled with a lifetime of January skies.
Despite their dimness, the stars
are still joined to the planets
by blurry equal signs. Venus in particular
is the colour of a blood cell
while the moon wears the face
of a seventeen-year-old boy.

I have always been a Capricorn, like
Mao Tse-tung, like Henry Miller,
like Jesus Christ. Always been
a mountain goat, believing in
heights. Patience, persistence
and other frugal forms of faith.

Astrology is destiny, so the Assyrians
said, their hearts black as
outer space. Fate: the speed
light travels as it hits the ground.
Pisces with her weedy brain. Leo
of the hackles and brows. Libra,
the identical thumbs. Once upon a star
the future knew what to expect.

In 1585, just as I was beginning to feel
hope, Sixtus V drew a wide black line
between the Italian Alps and the dazzling
horizon. *God, more holy*
than the Milky Way, is what he had
to say, *Christ the shepherd,*
not the goat. Free will spilling
the self into cracks and valleys.

Call me confused, like an ash,
or a blink. A Bible paperweight
holds down the centuries.
Even though the night sky has lost
most of its magic, those greedy
black holes, I still believe in the
unknown known, the sacred star.

SECTION 4

CORNWALL 1916

. . . what do I propose to do with the world? Sweep it all into one gloriously muddy pile of hothouse orchids and bamboo shoots, of kings and queens and porcelain Chinese dolls, of blood and pus, of thatched roofs and ivory towers, of porridge and ostrich eggs, of zippers and helium balloons, of snowy thighs and crimson bums, of *Childe Harold* and heroic couplets, of Goose Fair and Timbuktu, of coal dust and tsetse flies, all in one mountain of ooze. What then? I'll strike a measly match and *poof!* Isn't that what's meant when people say I want to set the world on fire? It's what I mean at any rate. A world come true in a column of smoke. The crimson ash of original man . . .

FREE RIDE

According to the vernacular,
that ancient language
of dropped dreams and broken shelves,
we are down and out.
Sixty-four cents
to every crumpled Uncle Sam.
A penny here, a penny there,
the north wind almost strong enough
for flying quarters.
No hope for windfalls or UFOs.
Hands thrown empty
in the Bay Street sky,
thin air sliced into shreds
of fear and despair.

Guilt over spendthrift flower beds
and next year's trip to Italy.
O economy! . . . desire's embodiment.
I see Giotto's wanton angels
and nothing less than Padua will do.
Bicycling past the Holland River
all I can think of
are expensive canoes.
Isn't a Gap T-shirt
somehow more exquisite
than a Fruit of the Loom?

I am poorly equipped
to censor the fuchsia
in their wicker baskets.
If only I was a red-winged blackbird,
even just one wing,
an all-out free ride.

According to life
being here is the only factor.
The voice on the radio
doesn't shudder
while reciting the latest
Albanian statistics,
hardly a tremor
when the old Nazi is shot in Paris,
barely a drop of adrenalin
at the mention of Yeltsin's spiralling health.

But the down-and-out dollar
shakes up such a storm,
my little patch of suburbia
registers on the Richter scale.
We are not afraid of volcanoes,
not afraid of Castro
or Contras, or *Candyman.*
Just a thirty-six-cent loss of self.

POSSIBILITIES . . .

AMERICA 1923

Strange, the Americans graft
themselves to crowded towns
generic cities. Glass eyes
afraid of shattering. They are
clinging to spring avenues
hugging creamy walls, pushing
outskirts further out. Pretending
the land no longer exists.

A land where people can
surrender to the blood, the
feuding seasons, where life basks
upon prehistoric rocks
rejoicing over opals of
sweat, flamingo feathers, flesh
reshaped by a squeeze of
August wind. America
sneaks itself on the world
like a treasure map. A land where
blood streams from the Rockies, splashing
over canyons and meadows
staining both the desert and
the sea with a suicidal
sunset; a land dying from
the sheer beauty of its
possibilities.

Summer faints amongst the holy pines.
Winter binds the valleys
in a grip of empty ice. And
through it all, abundant eyes: a field
of quartz, a million apple trees
a finger painting of
the Northern Lights. America
makes me sweat in its Everglades
take flight from its bleached abandoned
bones, breathe to the roar of
a waterfall. America
insists on surrender
bleeding me of normal vision.

THE MORNING DEVOURS

The wind shrieks up and down the house
like a predatory bird,
feathery swirls of dust
everywhere, snakes hitting blunt heads
on bedroom walls, the sun leaping
through windows like a tiger.

Another meat-eater of a morning,
soaked-up city teeming with clotheslines
and coffee smog, an itch in every
sweltering corner. Careful of those
mail slots, their sweaty discontent.
The cracks and cleavage of it all
coming down on our heads.

Think of what we've made for ourselves:
somewhere to escape from, shoes lined up
in neat little rows like jungle airstrips.
The walls are trembling, rugs coughing,
cellar stairs tumbling into one another
until there's no place else to go.

Is any of this free will?
Thick skulls with their dinosaur attitudes.
We settle on making the best of it,
stride into the sun and are instantly
ripped into shadows. Another day,
the six-sided die of a risk.

We don't remember choosing
any of these extremes: the sight
of ourselves in the bathroom mirror,
pyjama pants curling around ankles,
the parrot squawks of the *Globe and Mail*
with its daily dooms, the poem
that keeps misinterpreting.
On we go, all these wrists hailing cabs,
these hearts beating in a pile
like something the ants dragged home.
We are the everyday, stripped raw
with sun, blown up and down,
dust-snakes writhing in our lungs.

We choose, escaping on a daily
basis, with or without our feet,
shadows tattered and windy.
The morning devours our beliefs,
our cautions, splitting us into shrieks,
the sort of music you'd expect from bones.

TO WAKE THE DEAD

Comes the Father followed by
a cortège of sleepy sinners.
Stone-cold church gaping
like an empty tomb. Eyes steaming
in the stained glass light.

Death is said to slowly climb
the esophagus, disguised as
a kind of hunger for nothing
on earth. Premonitions of death
occur frequently on Sunday mornings,
the heart chilling to the hardness
of wood. Lips barely moving
as the Bible tells the future.
Time reflected on cathedral ceilings,
a constriction of clouds.

Father filled with salvation,
the present moment caught
in his throat. Bully this,
confess to that, he slaps
his congregation's soul
the way a surgeon beats
on a broken heart. *Careful,*
Christ is slipping away with
every undetermined breath. Sounds
like the world is bound to end
before the Sunday roast is even
browned. The only thing to do
is hold each muscle still, pretend
to be a pillar or a pew. Father's
voice passes over row on row, the
awful radar of an angel's sword.

How words can terrify. Speak of
God at the right moment
and the room will seethe
with everlasting dread. Father
never seems to stop and
swallow. His sermons hit the floors
and scale the walls. As if
he were trying to wake the dead.

EXTREME

Today, half-frozen, the blade of the wind
slices exclamation marks on my cheeks,
my body and the body of the birch tree
and the body of that
salt-stained aluminum fence
all one sheath of ice.
This is the only thought winter thinks
like the frost in an old refrigerator,
a bristle of cold white whiskers
poking into everything.
The thumbs of my gloves have been sucked stiff.
The sky, colour cloned from the fence.
Birches peel, lean toward
me, skin after skin of snow.

What a stem-winder this January is,
as close to a glacier as you can get
without being instantly embalmed.
Wool and rubber give no protection.
My down-filled vest might as well be stuffed with ice.
There are times and this is one of them
when it's smart to be inhuman.
Exquisite numbness, an eternal flame
frozen at the South Pole like a flag.

No *via media* for those of us
in the white dusk
who stand at the edges of parks and fields,
thinking about bootprints
disappearing into birches.
No way but forward, that determined
blizzard of extremes.
Ghosts walking through ghosts,
a cracked glass web of winter.

COUPLES

They're all murmuring, purling
like rivers – wives blowing up
balloons, husbands slow with their
pocketfuls of pins.

They're all whispering, launching
words, questions up, in the sky –
the girl raising her arms as
if flying a kite, the boy
with his muscles and rocks, both
trapped by the gravity of love.

And no one knows what they're
saying, whether sounds string
into sentences, whether
brains are really transmitting
or, could be, blocked by each other
like rooms clumsy with chairs.

What a life, this love – doesn't
touch the way they look, taste,
only their hearts contained like
darkness in the folds of sky.
Perhaps somewhere in a small
town, a desert island, there's
a lively woman, rapture
in the top of a tree, her
man lifting through branches
to the sun.

LIVING WELL

1. *The Front Page*

Oscar de la Renta and his wife Francoise
are smiling front page of the *New York Times*.
They are rich and living well.
I cut the page into random pieces, an eye,
a gold ring, a string of pearls, to see if fragments
of a smile can be rearranged into a frown.
But no, gold is gold, forced to gleam,
the worst I can make it resemble
is a small yellow dog lying on a red silk lap.
The only thing I can do with the pearls
is transform them into miniature eggs,
something a seahorse might deposit in a sapphire sea.
Their eyes are the pale green bubbles
crowning the tops of floodlit fountains.
Even the tiniest flecks of paper glitter in the dark.
There are so many synonyms for wealth and happiness.

2. *The Best Revenge*

Living well is still the best revenge,
how the *New York Times* sums up the richly grinning life.
Revenge, like silver pistols on black velvet,
like blood in crystal cups.
Notice how, when living well, everything
is one colour, nothing patterned, just blue skies
or wide green lawns. Notice even more the word
revenge hanging over the de la Rentas' heads
in a caption white on black. Revenge is almost
a lack of colour, in order to go with everything.
But revenge against what? In other pictures
not appearing in newsprint, we see Francoise tangled
in bed, choking a nightmare with a diamond collar.
Revenge. And there she is outdoors, trapping
November winds in antique Egyptian jars, rolling
dead leaves into Persian carpets. Oscar is seen
eating only foods made from Tibetan trances,
having wrinkles removed by million-dollar creams,
ordering bell jars placed on his shadow.
How dare death with its cheap rings on calloused fingers.
Revenge against the smallness of it all, the pinprick,
the air-eating aches, the spoonful of chills.
The de la Rentas fortify themselves with grandeur,
every sweeping gesture a pain flung to the stars.

WANTING HIM

This is how we want him: back sweaty
against the wall, arms flung, thighs
slightly trembling, spread too far apart.

Much more provocative than
body parts arranged neatly
in a wooden box, or puffs of
ash and bone cast into the wind.
Torso with just a little twist,
ribs enhanced, head slinking over
right shoulder, eyelids sultry.

If God expects to outshine
Colorado gun boys and Hollywood
candy, he'll have to advertise.
Vanity Fair, say, a thick, glossy
two-page spread, a pair of white tight
Calvins, trickles of oily sweat,
bottom lip loose and surly.
Grinning and baring, hair spiked
into exquisite black thorns.

An image worth paying for.
Imagine a glimmering red can
of Coke slipping through his fingers,
or an unlit Lucky Strike
tucked behind one ear. Picture
a pair of Brook Brothers shades
hiding his real feelings.
Is he enjoying the pain,
the notoriety? Is he bored
with all our lazy devotion?

Live for him, sleep with him, give him
all the credit. . . . The dusky blond
hairs on the small of his back
had better be glistening. The hard round
muscles of his upper arms,
exactly the right size for cupping.
And don't forget the upside down *V*
of his trembling thighs, like Cupid's arrowhead.

Rule #1: what we want will save us.
Lots of dollar bills, lots of creamy flesh,
lots of wet kisses. Lots of pictures
of him, to die for, the kind of guy
who even when he bleeds all over us
leaves only the faintest of magazine
smudges in the warm damp of our hands.

THE UNAVOIDABLE MAN

He is the brother-in-law who
sells life insurance, the high school
bully, the next-door neighbour
with a Black Sambo on his lawn.

His greetings bruise your upper
arms, his knowledge of hockey
numbs you. Such companionship:
candid farts and comedies
with the "little woman." The
subtlety of jabs and winks.

The guy belongs to everyone.
Like "Tie a Yellow Ribbon," he
repeats himself. Talks of cars as if
they were drugs. Brags about his boss,
bellows through his sleeves. Hollers in
the screen door, a giant water hose.

Come the family picnic,
the school reunion, the
barbecue. A basketball
to chase, retrieve. The ultimate
tale of last night's game. A
couple of gasps in the direction
of every woman's legs.

The guy and I wolf down our
paper plates, throw ourselves gassily
into conversation, take it
easy or whichever way we can.

In the dusk we trade stories
of skeet shoots and salmon streams,
killing mosquitoes and piling them
on the arms of our chairs.

FEELING THE POWER

Superman is frozen in the sky
like a bird in an ice storm, struggling
so hard to fly, to rescue each
and every one of us, that his fists
have knocked holes in the wind.
He has already wrestled with
all our other gods, and won,
both our joys and miseries
entirely our own. We seldom
notice the sky anymore, our necks
sore from lifting so much light,
from cradling telephones
and maintaining steady glares.

Facts and fantasies are one,
all for the best. As if Einstein
keeps an eye on us, fleeting
energies, measly matter. Faith
in the last-minute rescue,
the sky melting into the slither
of our skulls. Like that telephone
conversation, the air connecting
us, all those invisible thoughts.

Everyone falling from faith
as if from tall buildings. So
much disintegration, so many
needs, Superman bursting
from the centre of the earth.
Call it life or mortality, our bodies
rearranged, our hearts ending
up in our mouths. We are going
so fast, we've almost replaced
ourselves, the power lost
as it soars downwind.

LUCKY PIGS

– a pig's orgasm lasts thirty minutes.

The first thing he feels is a ripple,
tail teasing a tiny circle in his fur.
Foreplay, thrusts turning into tingles.
Then a shudder across the great expanse
of his belly, and back again.
Quivers, flutters, you name it,
down the barracuda bone of his spine,
twisting him like the rope of a tornado.
A minute and a half has passed.

Seconds later, he's tripping
through some imaginary meadow,
nice and mucky, bindweed
wrapped around his hooves.
He tumbles into a wet thatch of grass,
rolling toward the horizon, stones squealing
as he crushes them to dust.
A final tumble, flooding the sky with his
tremors. A five-minute world-quake.

This is enough to send a vegetarian
reaching for his gun. Bacon
sizzling, bacon steaming, bacon
shooting across the dusk
like a bloody comet.
He doesn't give a slime for anything
at the moment, but the moment itself,
shivers transforming his snout into sparks
of static, mud bursting into nude pink flames.

Ten minutes and his ears are undulating,
his eyeballs squirming in their sockets.
He isn't really a pig anymore
but an avalanche.
Fifteen minutes, he's well past
the point of metaphors.
No one who can hold a pen
has ever gone this far.
The farmer and his wife are sour spasms of envy.

Don't even think of it anymore,
pure pleasure gushing from tongue
to colon, all that happy shit.
The clock hits twenty
and the whole barnyard is swelling,
mud shooting up like Roman candles.
The chickens are quivering in their corners.
Cows spilling milk. Mice
making the haystacks twitch.

By the time half an hour has passed
the entire countryside reeks of sulphur and love.
There's a huge moon screaming over the treetops
and lots of silver rips in the sky.
All the females back in their pens,
sharing their sighs.
He snorts approval, twirls his tail
into a neat little jack-in-the-box,
baring his teeth on a stunned cob of corn.

LET THERE BE LIGHT

My purpose is laid out on the kitchen table:
cereal bowl and spoon, Arts Section
of the morning paper, CD case for
Count Basie Swings, Joe Williams Sings,
glasses waiting patiently for face.
Chair beams its empty square, searching
for my bum. Still life with incomplete.

*

I prayed last night, bless this, bless that,
before falling asleep and dreaming
about donkeys at Riverdale Farm.
Bale of hay, tub of water, they chanted,
all they lived for, all they required.
I instantly wrote a children's book,
God showing his gums and braying on every page.

*

Hope is the most stubborn part of me,
the last to wake up. It rubs its crumby eyes
and stumbles into the bathroom, peeing
down the outside of the toilet bowl,
forgetting afterwards to wash its hands.
It has scrambled eggs stuck between its teeth
for hours. It forgets to wear ankles and ears.

*

Believe in the mirror!
Memorize! Copy!

*

I wake up sleepwalking in the garden,
hip-deep in phlox and breeze.
For a moment I just stand there,
imagining my head as a blossom, something
beautiful and temporary.

*

Wake-up always starts with a nail file,
but soon turns into a long, slashing sword.
A pillow sliced in two, spilling all its two-bit fears.
One second I'm a severed limb, the next
a flashing blade. Breakfast with a stranger,
cutting bananas into round white screams.

THE WAITING ROOM

Waiting in a waiting room –
would-be nurses, waiters,
dignitaries, all of us
temporarily unemployed.
Waiting for miracles, you
know, a money tree, a
relationship. Some with
prayers as references, others
visual, the sucked-in hunger
of the streets.

One by one, we disappear,
a navy blue man
mispronouncing our names.

My heart is cracked, a
novelty bank. On good days
seven out of ten fingers
work. No need to fret,
I will not cry, but if
suddenly I cease to move,
touch me somewhere I would
never expect. There are two
sides to me, the past and this,
a pose to complement your hands.

As we wait, no one speaks,
like dishes in a rack. A
small display of talent, yes
one can read, another sweeps
shoulders in a glance. So neat,
I can talk to the pleat in my pants
or place a finger gently to my eye.

When my name is called
in tones of navy blue
I do not disappear but
merely change my seat, my room.

I think I shall become
a member of the human race, a
nickel branch or half
a conversation. Might you need
someone who can pray for profit,
who can feed the hungry with their
knees? Just temporary work,
waiting for the future.

THE WORKING DEAD

This is the realm of blind potatoes.
Ingrown afterlife: stuck here in grips
of gloves and garden tools, grasping
underground cables for filaments of warmth.

Maggot fear is luxury, as are
worms and suffocation. No one
is digging to Tibet. A mouthful
of loneliness, an incision of air.

The valour in death is inorganic.
Inside the machine: the tiny
courage of bolts and seeds. Rooted,
used, an eternal hum of grief.

Absorbing wars and feet, we are
the guts of tulips, of telephones
and beans. The foundation of now.
Shovels, vaults and dreams.

Here are the witch's ashes, cooled
and mixed with green forgotten gems.
Here are the lost cats, the basement
windows, the discarded carrot tops.

This is the land of bitter onions.
Crying upside down: forced to grow
your grass and graceless houses, grumbling
as your children high-rise closer to the clouds.

BLUE COLLAR

Lunch, a man sits hunched
in the cafeteria,
like bread folded over
a pale slice of cheese.

Counting sons, one by one, a twist of
knuckles trembling on the tabletop.

This is heroic, believe
it or not, a giant banner
in the bustling union hall.

All the working men – black thumbprints
in spongy bread. Their fathers buried
deep inside the stones of factory walls.

The lifeline in everyman's palm
a chain of worn-out days, a crevice
crawled by beads of sweat.

Let us have a lunch or
a love affair with the working
man. Let the body divide
like a hangnail, the heart
lodged swollen in the angry flesh.

A man stands upright through
the years, sons and banners hanging
from his aching arms. Bravado
more or less, a knife quivering
in a dirty wooden floor.

CROYDON 1909

. . . after a life of teaching row upon row of interchangeable boys, my corpse would be propped up against a blackboard, a textbook glued to stiff-clutched hands. Not the life for me: confident, talented and mad as I am. The educational system is primarily in place to teach restrictions and rules; think six inches at a time, conjugate your passions into a dozen harmless tenses, memorize borders and don't overstep, dream poetry that wouldn't offend a Sunday shoe. Small boys splintered into smaller men, so the world spins, like ants pushing a carousel. Is it arrogant that I will run away and write the sort of books that stall machinery? I must not mistake myself for brave, or other flatteries. A writer isn't a special case. Just an ornery ant, or wait, a cricket hatched by a family of black ants, an impossible worker who can't help but chirp at the first taste of dew, a singer of dark, grassy knells . . .

SOUNDINGS

This is the way sorrow should sound,
wind crazy with the dark,
cry of gulls bumping into planets,
hollow footsteps on the forest floor –
all the blind-eyed noises . . .
wilderness with the night
breathing through a microphone
of long and feeble skies.

This is the sound of sadness,
ghosts, loud and vivid dreams,
not our small talk, chatty
stars mumbling as if some pocket
of universe were boiling
like a pot of beans.
These conversations are nothing
but grey sky, monologues of
clouds drawn in pencil,
collage of black and white . . .
the bled-out rainbow at the end of grief.

This is the way we really sound,
inside those clouds
floating above the world,
a skin that insulates the soul . . .
the muffled bush below us,
dead flowers and animals
who have lost their tongues,
leaves without breeze,
the earth made of slippers.
No music, no speech.
The sky, like quiet
fingers, stopping our hearts.

A MILLION WORDS . . .
VENCE 1930

Seasons are arranged in a vase
by the window: a veil of violets
dusty daisies, a wrinkled-yellow
chestnut spray. Icicles grow clear
and thin, like magic flutes.

Phosphorus looks down upon us all
a crystal god who knows the shape of
marrow in our bones. Wind is to snap
us, rain to wilt. Sunlight needles.
Fingers digging fast, the ends of
earth, the glowing rock of graves.

What I will miss most about the world
is change. Introspective skies
suddenly catching sight of closed
umbrellas. Real flesh and blood
emerging from the sombre cells of
books. Women revealing their unexpected
selves. Someone else's death.

From this dying hand came the brandishing
of clouds and torches: a dream landscape
where meadows flourished under crops of
birds, spreading into continental shelves.
The birth of an ideal sustains the man
until both become a way of life; death
diminishing nothing but the self.

Years from here a stranger will walk
into my house, *the home of the infamous
etc.,* . . . claiming to feel my spirit
in the antique walls. Only the words
always wanting out.

The world of the dead is a megalopolis.
Shakespeare scrunched beside Wordsworth
who I could swear is almost sitting
on my knee. The combination of us all
will haunt you, the quantity.

I rush too far ahead, the daily world
peeling from my brain like cobweb.
All I seem to care about is living
not the life itself. The taste of water
rather than the soggy map. The sound
of words, touch of body hair, smell of
sea, look of mirrors. I will leave
nothing of myself behind, just these
second-hand sensations never quite complete.

The world is eternal, not the man.
I was something in the air, in the
rose bush: a spot of cold, a thorn.

Field upon field of daisies. Chestnuts
falling like a skyful of wish-wearied
stars. The countryside unconscious
with snow. The world is larger than
an eye or mouth, and death promises
to be fuller than even the greediest of
hands. I do not believe in puny ghosts
but in giant plans: a lifetime
that just might change the way
the world goes on alone.

SECTION 5

COMETS

One of those skies that makes the highway
feel all downhill, the colours of
a boudoir or a bruise. Cloud shapes
of sleeping polar bears and coiled
dragons, cold legends on the verge of blood.
Driving into it, symbols stretched
by a meaningless wind, our eyes
uplifted like those of grand mal saints.

The first orange gash, the size of a cat's
scratch, is mistaken for a plane.
A second, then a third, each aimed
south, three flaming tails. Comets
burrowing into the atmosphere.

Can't remember the last time the sky
was more than distance, a daze
of dumb blues and milky afterthoughts.
Something to crawl beneath, something
held above. Flushed, we search our brains
for comet trivia, mixing myth with
meteors, half-convinced that air can fall.

The highway hits a slope of the world's
incredible roundness, pointing the car
into a climb. A simple yellow
Chevette with wide eyes narrowing
into the thin lines of a gaze.
Driving up until we glare against
the electric heights of Toronto, where
comets burn holes in colourless towers,
headlights tunnel through solid stone.

AFTERLIFE . . .

THE ATLANTIC OCEAN 1925

Have you seen the way caterpillars
curl themselves in leaves?
So the ship rolls beneath wave after
wave. Wrapped in water, incomplete
our hands and feet disintegrate.
Splashily the afterlife unfolds.

Heaven is a coral reef where God
sits gingerly. Could that be the devil
stirring up the depthless muck?
Swim or fly, the eternal muscles
are the same. To spend what's left of me
afloat. A bitter salty spray.

WILD, WILD

Wild, how trees claw at one another,
rocks buried half-alive, spiders spitting
mid-air. We are not to confuse these wilds
with human pathology. Nor to let literature
weep pathetic. Wild is numb, is brainless.
Where nothing ever happens twice.

This tree is a wooden cell; it knocks
in the wind and grows. This rock is a mineral
deposit. And the spider, the most alive
we'd say (like us), is a dark enzyme
oozing in the so-called light. A man may walk
through these wilds, or he may not.
If a poet, he will probably want to tell:
the same weeping willow again and again.

Numb is somehow tender to the touch – moss,
bark, breeze. A beautiful brainless rock,
the act of sitting an act of love.
Each soft spider dashing the wrist
brings one thrill of skin alive.

Wild, how trees touch back, rocks
muscle into open hands, spiders land.
A man sits confused in the forest,
pathetically talking to himself.
Everything feels and can't forget.

All men are pathological. Weeping,
they bring the adjectives down.
Always another man, half-awake, dangling
in the air. This is man's makeup,
the literature of all kinds.
The same man tough as trees, deep
as rock, spitting dreams. *Wild*,
he says. Wild.

A RECURRING LIFE

Born

> Born in the small change of winter hay,
> just another slushy footprint.
> Unbelievable, son of talent,
> miracle boy, body sinking
> in a drift of dirty snow, eyes
> as blurred as stars. Lies
> whimpering at the sky, cross-eyed,
> the sun burning way above him
> like a piece of wood. Listening
> to the long, sharp sobs of icicles
> melting in the manger doorway.

Living

> Will live in barns, or olive groves,
> or spare bedrooms, with sheep, with shade,
> with fevered women. He can fit himself
> just about anywhere, like DNA
> in a drop of blood. There's his pointy chin
> behind the sandstorm of a chainsaw,
> his forehead reflected in his mother's
> meagre wedding band. There he is,
> dangling from the points of a perfect stranger's
> heart. He's singing songs about thorns
> and grace, growing up to die like the rest of us.
> He's shape-shifting, or is that just
> another word for trying to please?
> His would-be wives can't keep him
> in one place, so forget him. All alone,
> his hands are others, lovers, thieves.

Word

The Word, a drawbridge out of order,
endless ups and downs. Talk, talk, everything
from performing waves to poison kisses,
dust genies billowing in the air
with their showy omens. What we have here
are the syllables of a man
bleeding adjectives like *gruesome* and *doubtful*.
The Bible opens like magician's doors,
revealing a pair of sandals,
a crown of thorns, a gold cross
swinging in the air. And for our next trick:
a shower of spit, an apple tree
sprouting all the synonyms for red.

Dying

You need to be ill sometimes, to lie
up there on the moon and moan something
pale and full of pity. You need to
shut off the TV, stretch out on the couch
and let the darkness fold its grieving arms
across you. You need to open
all the doors, middle of November,
letting in the children who have no faces
or homes, answering their questions
with a shiver. You need to climb up
on a thunderstorm roof, feel the lightning
shoot from your fingertips
as it burns fear into tiny worms of smoke.

Afterlife

In Anglican gardens, the pansies
have kitten faces, gussied up
in little bishop's robes. The Brethrens
don't bother with seeds or toys, just
unwatered, unweeded earth, patches
of the invisible. The agnostics
plant useful things like string and books
of matches. Are those Catholics
wading through fields of golden wheat,
or just hungry Unitarians?
Are you an atheist if you're found
in bed alone? Followers of
talent, sons of the wind with your babbling
tongues, your Advent calendars,
your horse-and-buggies. It's impossible
to even move without making
some kind of spiritual commitment.

Recurring Dream #1

Red-rimmed eyes glow in the dark kitchen.
You think of throwing a sponge at them,
flinging open the refrigerator
and freezing them in the shocking light.
But no matter what you do, they follow
your every move. Salvation is never
far away, a glance or two, like having
a vision sitting on your shoulder.

Recurring Dream #2

Wide awake, stoned on sheer will, Christ
the idea, dreaming of ways
to stop the darkness, pacing the garden,
walking the blooms one last time before bed,
breathing out great clouds of light.

MY NIGHTS ARE TAKEN UP WITH STARS

I dream I am standing on a dark hill,
land invisible below me, my only knowledge
the shape of other distant hills gesturing
through glints of moon. Looking up,
anticipating blackness, the odd star or two,
the sky is shimmering with light.

There has never been such a starry night before.
Or if there was, I was kneeling on the floor,
eyes shadowed in a crown of hands.
Many dreams have used me, falling
from ladders, nervous flights, walls pressing
close like bones from my own body. All with eyes
averted, closed, focused on myself.

Now my nights are taken up with stars,
with windy skies of silver wheat, with
narrow strands of dark like crows asleep.

A dream can change your life, any kind of vision
a vow, a promise of patient lungs, of hands
lifted above the head, above the body-self,
a knowledge of wasted dark.

Looking up at myself, my outstretched hands
are tossing bones through light
and for once, it's the bones dissolving.
My heart breathes hard, inflamed,
no need for fearing sleep, or death.
Look, my fingertips are wheat.

IN AN INSTANT

David, son of Michelangelo,
was for one moment a son of God.
Standing silently in a gallery,
smoothly strong and contemplative,
pale. At times as if enchanted.

Simply say David believes in beauty.
Fingers passed through candles
in gleams of blood and marble nails.
Believes in confidence and honesty,
patient stone, slow water, the wind's
inspiring ability to take the shape
of tent or shadow, bone or fatherhood.

Some might say he believes in death,
on show, the voyeurism of anatomy.
Or doubt, arms petrified in the abyss
of second thoughts. Even faithlessness,
primer boy overpowered by a frightening
world, helpless, will stand and stand, will stare.

Michelangelo would say David
believes in everything, in pumice stone,
raw wheat and thunder, in morning glory
mesmerized by frost, has sensed his face
sketched in student notebooks,
felt the shine of crowds turn dim, away,
known probing fingers, perchance a pulse,
outlasted touring days and fleeting eyes,
obsessive burying of flesh and earth.

David, flawless record of beauty, son
of momentary son of God, believes
in heaven on earth, the body relumed
each day of death. David dies and
lives through centuries, splendid
in the bloody reincarnation of the sun.

David believes himself to be the son
of Michelangelo. Michelangelo the man.
Although he's unable to see, he recalls
arms struggling with his arms, feels
his breast pressing on a softer breast.
Michelangelo went to heaven for an instant,
David holds him in a perfect marble fist.

CASA LOMA

The wind motivates men to build
monuments, hearts full
of gusty love. Their very breath
creates castles. One woman rose
every morning to a world of
turrets and stony splendour, of
repetitive birds doing ritual
dances on the wide wet lawn.
Her happiness, a flag waving
out the bedroom window.
The servants made soup from
her grateful tears, selling it
at the gates as magic.
And when the woman died
everyone wanted in, greedy
tourists rushing for souvenirs
of bottled air. People roamed
the rooms, listening to silly
stories some actor's voice was
always reciting. They half-
heard, (noisy gossips) chatting
about soap operas, reprimanding
children. No respect for
ghosts. No awe of castles.
Their covetous souls whisked
around as if they were at a shopping
mall. But at night, when the rooms
were empty, fat old spirits swept
away footprints. The woman wrote

entire diaries about how lonely
it was to be dead. Wrote away
the dross of each day, tossed it
out one of the many windows.
But of course men were never to
return. She sat, glowing, in her
old bedroom, behind the rope
that kept the crowds away.
There were no birds on the dark
lawn, just shadows she
imagined to be feathers.
She sat at the window, making no
reflection, shining out into the dark
like a light left on or a trick
the wind was playing with the moon.

LAST LIGHTS . . .

VENCE 1930

These days the sun is carted in
from a stagnant horizon
Aldous and Maria lifting
alongside the peasants; with
raised arms they urge the light against
my window, making me want to
believe the sky has stumbled
almost into my hands.

I am always competent to
see – my eyes, such blazing
window frames. Though my ankles
hesitate, though my heart hides
beneath a tomb of ribs, though my
head is shovel-heavy, I
insist to see: these walls as white
as virgins, that orange cat leaping
into Frieda's multicoloured
lap, those books gleaming
like underwater rocks
on the table a lifetime away.
Look at the blue vase, the
purple flowers: a bruise
arranged in a glimmer.

Strange how I – blood and earth and
thumbs – have become colourless
a piece of timid crystal
glaring down from a mantel.
In this kindly light I am weak
with rainbows. On Frieda's lips
I am something deep and pink.
Next to a pot of ink I am
a robin's egg. Only in the dark
am I dull and watery
the colour of a window
with the shade drawn fully down.

No energy to save this
savage world. Black deserts will
remain heartless. Grey men
simply stay grey. To be
happy now is to watch a tanned
boy change the shape of the sea.
Even the cat with its silly
bits of string, its dreams of
embraceable birds, has too much
purpose for me. I watch
a corner of the bed vanish
in the blinding yellow noon.

Each breath as long as a year.
The world lengthens into evenings.
My feet seem far away.
Vence, pretty villa.
Frieda looks to the south, nothing
but the edges of waves. Yet
another day outlasted, the
sun buried in fields of clouds.

Who presses the moon against
my window? Something oozing from
a rotten sky. Huxley, words are
finally beyond us.
Maria, pages are falling
on my eyes. In the rocking chair
Frieda knits the horrid white pus
the orange cat dangling from her lap.

TIMOTHY FINDLEY'S BOOTS, STONE ORCHARD SALE, OCTOBER 1998

She was looking for something richly personal:
a maroon velvet bathrobe
or a volume of Chekhov's stories,
snatches of dialogue underlined in pink.
She was looking for necessary, for loved:
a stuffed tiger with a tail stroked to shreds
or a pair of cashmere gloves,
fingerprints almost worn through.
How could she not be disappointed
by all the crockery and linen, anonymous clutter.
She was looking for the smudge
of a kiss on a wineglass,
a cat hair dangling from a blue paisley scarf.

When she sees the boots, *his* boots,
a shiver runs down the backs of her kneecaps,
ankles like knives sliding into the nerves of her feet.
She glides across the lawn,
thinking about toes, *his* toes,
still scrunched into their rubber nests.
The first thing she wants to do
is reach inside, retrieve the prize,
but no, how silly, ghost toes at best
just the vaguest hint of a wiggle.
She pauses, faking nonchalance,
then slips off her black Chinese slippers,
bare feet insolent and determined.

Why, hello there, Mr. Findley, her big toe
exclaims, the puddle of red polish like a come-on.
Squeezing her heel
against the memory of his.
As close to stealing a soul
as you can get in public.
And to think, she was looking for something
tasteful, a monogrammed handkerchief
or a signed book of poems by Phyllis Webb.
She had never dared to dream herself
standing in his footsteps,
imaginary mud oozing
warm against her skin.

She shuffles to a nearby bench,
the boots one slip behind her.
A poem is already spilling out
as she burrows in her bag for pen and pad.
"Tiff Findley's Boots," she'll call it,
overflowing with flesh and familiarity.
It will go nicely with the one about touching
Margaret Atwood's embroidered handbag at
Harbourfront.
I wade deep inside him, she scrawls,
words gobbling up the white page.
While across the lawn
another woman finds the Chinese slippers.
What small feet he has, she begins to compose.

A THOUSAND CUSHIONS

World update: encephalitis
claims another brain in Peru
while the streets of Des Moines, Iowa

flow like Parisian sewers.
Just another Sunday afternoon,
the earth throwing a hurly-burly

in Guam, the Body bleeding into
Africa, the poet and his wife
out shopping for a sofa.

A newsman says, two million,
a salesman, $799.
Rows and rows of leather, chintz,

cotton twill. Southwestern,
vanilla, William Morris vines.
A thousand cushions

to pamper our bones.
Do you have this in gold?
a Filipino family asks.

Loveseats beckon,
cushions soft as flesh.
Sectionals to rearrange us

until we're out of breath.
An easy chair numbing
the whole of my spine.

Will it float? I almost ask,
bulletproof, built-in brave?
Will it hold me as I die,

I mean really hold me?
Wanting so much to buy
a little peace, beyond it all.

Update, north Toronto: man
disappears in blue-striped couch,
no bother, no casualties.

LAST EVENING IN SIBERIA

We spent last evening in Siberia,
that coupling of distant Jack
and wind-chill wife, their
silver wedding bands gleaming
across the table from us
like tiny lifebuoys carved from ice.
Alone, Jack might be mistaken
for an island, nothing barren or
extreme, just some ink-blot piece
of rock riding the valleys of waves.
And his wife would probably be
more seasonal on her own, at worst
one of those anonymous cities
where weather is a fashionable excuse
for never stopping to chat.
But together, an explosive frost,
Jack and bride scraped by the same
north wind, shorelines and busy streets
blurred together in a tailspin.

As for me, I come from somewhere
like Switzerland, a combination
of my mother's politeness and my
father's fear of everyone else.
Their bodies collided like church bells,
once, twice, before they abandoned their bones
to become sheer music, harmony nearly
starving in the thin mountain air.
If it hadn't been for the Sicily
of my hot-tempered uncle and aunt,
I might never have learned to breathe,
great gusts of self and desire
blowing all those idle pleasure crafts
out onto the simmering turquoise seas.

Years later, a dot on the map myself,
I'm still overly sensitive to place, often
forced to flee those old Communist regimes
some friends think of as relationships.
So where am I now that I'm part of a *we*,
now that I've dropped my clean and quiet
neutrality? Am I half a sunset, a time
zone, a chestnut tree split down the middle
by a slice of lightning? Am I every
second footprint on a Caribbean beach?
A stream of one-way London traffic?
There are times when our convergence
feels like a trouble spot, somewhere
the River Styx and the River Eden cross.
We've even had our cold snaps in Siberia.
Most days though, we still feel undiscovered,
like a planet science hasn't got to yet
with its satellites and Richter scales.

LEAPS

July 20th, 1999, America huddles
around blurry black-and-whites
of the moon, team spirit flickering
in faded eyes. Once upon a time, 1969,
the whole damn galaxy fit on the tip
of a TV antenna, darkness
finally brought down to size.

How early is it in this first day
of the human race, have we touched
our toes and brushed our teeth?
More planets to discover than we can dream,
anniversaries of when we still believed
in leptons, valentines and God,
the moon archaic as a wagon train.

So proud of our first steps,
D-Days and *Jurassic Park*s,
the mind laced with Instant Grow
as the universe spasms and expands.

Calendars black with birthdays and other giant leaps,
from heart transplants in South Africa
to body parts in a Milwaukee fridge.
Horology is the new religion, ways to
divide eternity into feats and shocks.

On July 20th, 2029, will paeans be sung
for the discovery of sulphur gas on Jupiter,
for the birth of someone we haven't
even heard of yet, for the last time
we really looked at the moon?

DEL MONTE RANCH, QUESTA, NEW MEXICO 1924

. . . here where I first really noted how darkness doesn't fall at all, but devours. Like a cold mouth calling low from the clouds: this is the moment the world will end. It consumes our weakling faith, gobbles down our flickering eyes, licks us up as if we were tiny puddles. Frieda always slips inside the cabin just as the sun is about to be sucked from the sky, while I walk out to where the alfalfa field will be swallowed and watch as the darkness feeds on the hills. The pines and the firs are the first to go black. Then the aspens and cottonwoods: trees ten times my size gulped in a flash. The scrub-oaks seem to bleed before they disappear, bloodstains on the rocks. And then it comes for me, my feet tangled in the grass. Deliriously, I want to run, bound over those last sips of light. But I close my eyes, remain, solid as any tree, knowing that when I look again, the darkness will be everything, everywhere, and I no more than an alfalfa seed stuck between cold teeth. It's strangely peaceful to be so much a part of a demolished world. I feel my blind way back to Frieda, blending in with her invisibly . . .

AN OCCASIONAL THANKS

The dimmer switch dialled low, Ella Fitzgerald
on the stereo, our conversation easing *ritardando*
where even the smallest of words glow.
I give thanks for Thanksgiving, a good excuse
to fill the house with gourds and friends.
Just look at the way that well-worn carpet
gobbles up those crumbs. Feel the bookshelves
breathe in laughter, page after page of
tickled thumbs. Ever notice how Van Gogh's
stars are really pumpkins, how stroking a cat
will carry your warmth to the next lap,
how mashed potatoes taste like clouds. How
the world winds down to the keenness of a savour.

When dinner is done, dining-room table stripped,
last car rolled down the driveway, I wait
for the walls to groan or the couch to shift
in sudden dejection. After all, this is time,
the best and then the end. I expect the gourds
to turn bizarre, fruit of a nuclear blast.
Or the paper plates to biodegrade
right before my eyes. I can't help feeling
friendship is just an occasion, something to
wear down the carpet, pat the cat, stop
negligence from blurring me beyond recognition.

The morning after is always glaring, children shrieking
through the streets, tearing off words like ears
or thumbs. If my heart were suddenly to slow,
then stop, no one would even know. My cats
would continue nibbling the dining-room carpet,
my books carrying on with their circular selves.
In the harsh ordinary sun, everything Van Gogh painted
resembles a hole, naked light wrenched of its heat,
where even a cup of tea tastes like smog.

Sometimes Ecclesiastes says it all, a time for
great and sad, a wearing down of everything.
Seems there is even time to start again,
stringing Christmas lights round and round
the house, buying ornaments and angel hair.
I think I'll invite my rare friends to celebrate,
breathing them in until my heart is warm
and whole. A time for luxurious occasions
in between the blurs and groans.

MAPMAKING

Gunshot syllables: the rhythm of anthems,
islands shouting from ragged shores.

Virtue is a man who shoots only at strangers.
Be it squares, lots or maps, someone will eventually
stir the grass. The trespass of wanderlust.

Dirt is a real prize. And roots.
The wind puffs along the hairline, parting
the brain into two camps. Blasted hills.

Pastures repel pastures, rivers split
and mountains implode into caves.

The world is a self-delusion, sustained.
The world is a floating footprint,
a shadow men fall for.
Countries of mine and moss, of clutched air.

Such is the war between shut-ins and
those exposed on the barbed-wire fence.
They are fighting for the rights to snowfalls.
Sunlight squatters. The realm of a glance.

ACKNOWLEDGEMENTS

My first gratitude, of course, goes to those editors and publishers who initially saw merit in my previous books: Guernica Editions, Quarry Press, Brick Books, Empyreal Press and St. Thomas Press, with a special note of thanks to Allan Brown, Antonio D'Alfonso, Bob Hilderley, David Kent, Don McKay and Sonia Skarstedt.

And even before the books, heartfelt appreciation to all the literary magazines who gave clean, white pages to my work, an encouragement that was truly inspiring. Some of the New Poems have previously appeared in *The Antigonish Review, Arc, Grain, Larger Than Life* (Black Moss Press), *Matrix, Prairie Fire, Quarry* and *Why I Sing the Blues* (Smoking Lung Press). "Knee-High" won second prize in the 2002 Petra Kenney Poetry Competition.

A thousand thanks to Brian Bartlett, Glenn Hayes and Robert Hilles who took the time and energy to advise me on these selections, making what seemed like an impossible process not only doable, but thoroughly enjoyable. Thanks too to Silas White whose vision and direction were invaluable ingredients throughout. Special mention to Don Domanski, Pat Jasper and Isabelle Saunders for their constant support and encouragement over the years. And most of all, deepest love and recognition to Karen Dempster: muse, maverick and best of everything.

BOOKS BY BARRY DEMPSTER

TITLE INDEX